Ana Kokkinos

Ana Kokkinos

An Oeuvre of Outsiders

Kelly McWilliam

EDINBURGH
University Press

For Lewis

Edinburgh University Press is one of the leading university presses in the UK. We publish academic books and journals in our selected subject areas across the humanities and social sciences, combining cutting-edge scholarship with high editorial and production values to produce academic works of lasting importance. For more information visit our website: edinburghuniversitypress.com

We are committed to making research available to a wide audience and are pleased to be publishing Platinum Open Access editions of the ebooks in this series.

Edinburgh University Press Ltd
The Tun – Holyrood Road
12(2f) Jackson's Entry
Edinburgh EH8 8PJ

Typeset in 12/14 Arno and Myriad by
IDSUK (DataConnection) Ltd, and
printed and bound by CPI Group (UK) Ltd, Croydon, CR0 4YY

A CIP record for this book is available from the British Library

ISBN 978 1 4744 4052 3 (hardback)
ISBN 978 1 4744 3109 5 (webready PDF)
ISBN 978 1 4744 3107 1 (paperback)
ISBN 978 1 4744 3110 1 (epub)

Contents

Figures

Acknowledgements

The idea of writing this book was conceived while preparing a paper for the 2015 conference of the Film and History Association of Australia and New Zealand (FHAANZ), so I am grateful to the conference organisers and my fellow presenters for the inspiration they provided. This book would not have been possible, however, without the support of the University of Southern Queensland and, in particular, the study leave which afforded me the opportunity to dedicate time and attention to the project. I am grateful to the University of Southern Queensland for this opportunity and to my colleagues and students who supported my work during this time, particularly Andrew Hickey and Rachael Wallis who covered my teaching. I also want to acknowledge the USQ Librarians, who are a phenomenal team and were a terrific support to this research. Thank you also to Malcolm Brown, Lisa French, Dominique Henry, Laurie Johnson, Joanna McIntyre, Rhod McNeill, Matt Nielsen, Mark Ryan, and Erica Smith for your support and/or guidance, and Sharon Bickle for reading an early draft and contributing to Chapter 3. And to my family, who offered their support: much love to Stuart, Helen, Blake, Harvey, M'ley, Sean, and, of course, Lewis.

I would also like to thank the reviewers for their helpful feedback on the initial proposal and the series editors, Lucy Bolton and Richard Rushton, for their guidance on the full draft. Particular thanks must go to Edinburgh University Press, and specifically Gillian Leslie and Richard Strachan for their supportive stewardship of the project from beginning to end, and to Rebecca Mackenzie, for her work towards the book design. It was a delight and a privilege to work with you all.

Finally, thank you also to Taylor & Francis Ltd. Chapter 3 was repurposed from an earlier article originally published as:

McWilliam, Kelly and Sharon Bickle (2017), 'Re-imagining the rape-revenge genre: Ana Kokkinos' *The Book of Revelation*', *Continuum: Journal of Media and Cultural Studies* 31.5: 706–13, <http://dx.doi.org/10.1080/10304312.2017.1315928>.

It is reprinted by permission of the publisher (Taylor & Francis Ltd, http://www.tandfonline.com).

One thing is for sure: you don't ever forget the films of Ana Kokkinos.

(Free 2016)

Introduction: Ana Kokkinos

I first watched a film directed by Ana Kokkinos during my doctoral research. I was investigating recently released films with women directors and lesbian protagonists as part of a larger survey of 'lesbian romantic comedies' and it was during that research that I first saw *Only the Brave* (1994).[1] Though by no means a romantic comedy – Kokkinos has joked that she will make a comedy 'when [she] grow[s] up' (qtd in Buckmaster 2009: n.p.) – it was a striking and unusual film that stayed with me, not least as a young queer woman growing up in suburban Australia. Indeed, as I contend in Chapter 1, *Only the Brave* was the first queer coming-of-age film in Australia, and one of the first in the world to feature a queer girl.[2] But unlike other queer coming-of-age films that tended to privilege 'positive and compassionate attitudes' (Padva 2004: 357), Kokkinos instead explores the alienation, estrangement, and visceral distresses of those outside the mainstream. Her oeuvre has been described as 'about as confrontational as Australian films get' (McFarlane 2010: 86) and 'among the most hard-hitting bodies of work in Australian cinema' (Buckmaster 2014: n.p.). More than that, though, Kokkinos's oeuvre is a body of work at once both distinctive and culturally significant, and warranting considerably more attention than it has yet received. And it is to that broad project that this book aims to first contribute.

The director

Ana Kokkinos (1958–) is an Australian screenwriter, producer, and director best known for her work directing fictional films, including the short *Antamosi* (1991), short feature[3] *Only the Brave* (1994), and features *Head On* (1998), *The Book of Revelation* (2006), and *Blessed* (2009). Alongside her work in fictional film, Kokkinos has directed multiple episodes of popular Australian television dramas and docudramas, from *Eugenie Sandler P.I.* (2000) to *Seven Types of Ambiguity* (2017–),[4] as well as co-directed the documentary *The Original Mermaid* (2002) with Michael Cordell. With a body of work spanning almost three decades, Kokkinos is one of Australia's most distinctive filmmakers, not least with her sustained focus on the city of Melbourne (the setting of all of her fictional films) and her visceral depictions of 'outsiders' (two points to which I return). She is also one of the country's most celebrated filmmakers. Her films have premiered at the Director's Fortnight at the Cannes, Venice, Toronto, and San Sebastian film festivals; won more than thirty awards nationally and internationally; and been praised by scholars and critics alike (Kokkinos n.d.). She has been described as, among other things, 'a major talent' (McFarlane 2010: 87), a 'celebrated' filmmaker (Buckmaster 2009: n.p.), an 'acclaimed director' (Ross 2012: 51), and a 'filmmaker in powerful command of the medium' (Hopgood 2009: 35) with 'a body of work that makes a significant contribution to global cinema' (French 2013: n.p.).

Yet Kokkinos very nearly wasn't a filmmaker at all.

One of three daughters, Kokkinos was born in Yarraville, Victoria on 3 August 1958, three years after her Greek parents migrated to Australia (Kalina 2009). As a working-class Greek-Australian girl growing up in the western suburbs of Melbourne – 'the only Greek family in an Irish working-class street' (Kalina 2009: n.p.) – the idea of becoming a filmmaker felt 'remote, it just didn't feel like a career prospect' (Kokkinos qtd in Barber 1998: 5). Certainly it was not the career she initially pursued. Kokkinos graduated from Monash University in 1982 and worked in industrial law for close to a decade. It was in that capacity that she worked alongside future Australian Prime Minister Julia Gillard at Slater & Gordon (Kent 2010: 73), with both young lawyers sharing a keen interest in social justice (Kalina 2009), a preoccupation that resonates in Kokkinos's films. But where Gillard was joining the firm in 1987, Kokkinos was soon to leave. Perhaps ironically, it was the offer of a partnership at her law firm that motivated her departure (Kalina 2009). Kokkinos has said of the time:

> I got to a point in my law career where I realised that I should make the break, either I committed myself to the law or said I really want to become a film-maker, I really want to become a director. I'll give it a go and see what happens. And that's virtually what I did. I threw everything in and applied to film school. (Kokkinos in Malone 1999: n.p.)

Indeed, in 1990 Kokkinos completed a course run by Women in Film and Television (WIFT), which, as its name suggests, aimed to bring more women into filmmaking in Australia (Barber 1998: 5). And, with Kokkinos, it succeeded. In 1991 Kokkinos was accepted into a one-year postgraduate filmmaking course at Swinburne Film and Television School (which became the Victorian College of Arts or VCA), in part through the two short films she made during her WIFT course (Katsigiannis 1998), and graduated the following year at thirty-four years of age. Kokkinos has described entering filmmaking later in life as 'a very active conscious decision to say, "I now feel stronger and in a better position to launch into something like this"' (qtd in Barber 1998: 5).

Now almost three decades since the release of her first film, this is the first monograph to focus on the director. In doing so, I focus specifically on Kokkinos's fictional oeuvre comprised of *Antamosi, Only the Brave, Head On, The Book of Revelation*, and *Blessed*. Kokkinos's films, though not previously the focus of a book, have nevertheless been widely reviewed, particularly in the Australian and queer press, and are, to a lesser extent, the focus of journal articles and book chapters. While scholars have long drawn attention to the marked paucity of scholarship on the director (Hardwick 2009; Collins and Davis 2004; Berry 1999), reasons for which I point to later, the work that does exist on Kokkinos nevertheless offers valuable insights and an important starting point. Thus far, the majority of existing scholarship focused on Kokkinos has centred on *Head On* and often been interested in aspects of the depiction of either queerness (Hunn 2000; Jennings and Lominé 2004; Vernay 2006; McIntyre 2010), ethnicity (Conomos 2014; Plunkett 2006; Aquilia 2001; Bennett 2007; Freiberg and Damousi 2003), or both (Tziallas 2010; Papanikolaou 2009; O'Regan 2001). Considerably less scholarship has investigated Kokkinos's other films, though of the work that does, much of it is interested in Kokkinos's use of genres, and particularly the intersections between genre, gender, and/or sexuality (for example, McWilliam and Bickle 2017; Henry 2014; Heller-Nicholas 2011a, 2011b; Hopgood 2009; Hardwick 2009).

Though diverse foci are inevitably taken within this body of scholarship, these broader trends nevertheless point towards the noteworthiness of Kokkinos's privileging of difference in a national cinema that has historically 'been overly concerned with the fabrication of a metonymic Australian masculinity' and 'ethnic and racial exclusiveness' (Craven 2001: 6), which have been enunciated through the 'white, heterosexual man of Anglo-Irish origin as the Australian type par excellence' (Seco 2008: 145). In contrast, all but one of Kokkinos's films centre around working-class, first- or second-generation Greek immigrants who are often also young and/or queer. Notably, these are characteristics the director largely shares: Kokkinos has discussed being a lesbian, second-generation Greek immigrant, who grew up in a working-class family in the western suburbs of Melbourne (Thomas 1999; Kalina 2009). While Kokkinos has stated that her films are not 'autobiographical', she has nevertheless described them (and particularly *Only the Brave*) as being 'born out of [her] own experiences' and part of a desire to bring something resembling her own lived experiences to the screen (in White and Lambropoulos 2017).

And indeed Kokkinos's fictional films, too, are all shot and set in the port city of Melbourne, the capital city of Victoria and the city in which Kokkinos still resides, and often specifically in the western suburbs in which she grew up. While her decision to consistently film in Melbourne presumably speaks partly to issues of convenience and finance, it is also the Australian city most associated with immigrants and Greek immigrants in particular. Melbourne has been a 'sister city' of the Greek city of Thessaloniki since 1984, for instance, in recognition of Melbourne's role as 'home to the largest Greek-speaking population outside of Europe' ('Greece' 2018). Well-known for its 'Greek precinct', Melbourne is also the site of a new 'Global Greek Diaspora Library' being built in collaboration with the National Library of Greece (Ioannou 2017). But unlike Sydney, which is frequently associated on film with iconic images of the internationally recognisable Sydney Harbour Bridge or Sydney Opera House, there are 'few dominant or defining images of Melbourne' in much Australian cinema outside of 'fleeting images of the skyline and muddy Yarra River' (Danks 2012: 6). Instead, Melbourne-set cinema is frequently 'representationally heterogeneous' and 'spatially indistinct' (Danks 2012: 6), a kind of 'non-place' (Danks 2017: n.p.). The diverse, indistinct Australian city functions emblematically of Australian society more broadly, but also introduces themes of 'place and placelessness, home and homelessness' (to adapt Craven 2001: 8), and insiders and outsiders.

Lisa French – who represents an important precedent for the present study as the first to discuss Kokkinos's fictional oeuvre (2012, 2013) – notes:

> The cinema of Melbourne film-maker Ana Kokkinos [...] offer[s] an *insider's* view of place. Yet these insiders are also outsiders who are frequently 'Othered', painfully aware of their difference due to their sexuality (as gays or lesbians); their ethnicity (as Greek immigrants within a troubled multicultural Australia); their socio-economic status (as working class, and often disenfranchised youths); and their place as sons and daughters battling familial tensions (particularly as second generation migrants). (French 2012: 66)

The idea of the outsider in the work of Kokkinos is thus a focus I draw from French. I elaborate on it briefly below before expanding on it throughout this book.

The outsider

For celebrated film critic David Stratton (2017), 'stories of outsiders are an enduring theme of Australian cinema' (and, indeed, of many cinemas and cinematic genres around the world). For Stratton (2017), stories of outsiders in Australian cinema revolve around 'strangers from other places coming to, surviving, and adapting to an unknown land' as well as the 'inner mental struggle we [all] face to fit in and belong'. These enunciations of the outsider inevitably take numerous forms across the different genres and styles of Australian cinema, though 'a significant proportion of Australian features since 1970' articulate this relationship to the land vis-à-vis 'the bush', and often through a white male seeking to 'tame' or survive the land (Raynor 2000: 118; Craven 2001). In contrast, Kokkinos's cinema is intimate and psychological in focus, transposing the 'survival' and 'adaptation' of her outsiders to exclusively urban and suburban spaces that often symbolise the interiority of those outsiders (French 2012, 2013): abandoned shacks, urban back alleys, run-down houses in outer suburbs – sites isolated from mainstream society.

Outside *The Book of Revelation*, these outsiders are, as French (2012) noted earlier, typically multiply marginalised as working-class, first- or second-generation Greek immigrants dealing with familial conflict, who are often also young and/or queer. In fore-grounding multiple axes of difference and the relational overlapping of them – such that the experience of women, for example, is also 'shaped by other dimensions of their identities, such as race and class' (Crenshaw 1991: 1242) – Kokkinos takes an intersectional approach to her depiction of the outsider in much of her oeuvre (Brah and Phoenix 2004; Phoenix and Pattynama 2006). Much of Ari's conflict with his father in *Head On*, for instance, revolves specifically around the tension between his gender and ethnicity, as a young Greek man expected to marry a woman and start a family, and his sexuality as a non-monogamous queer. In often underscoring the intersectionality of her outsiders, Kokkinos emphasises the outsider as the sum of complex, socio-culturally situated, and 'shifting configurations of inequality along various dimensions' (Atewologun et al. 2016: 224). Where Kokkinos does employ a hegemonic protagonist – as with the white, hetero-masculine Daniel in the seemingly atypical *The Book of Revelation* – he undergoes a traumatising abduction that forcibly repositions him as an outsider to his own life, concluding the film literally removed from mainstream society by being arrested and in police custody.

Kokkinos's outsider, then, is a motif through which themes of alienation, disaffection, and the powerlessness of the marginalised are explored, typically through a visceral depiction of the experience of trauma. Key examples of these traumatic experiences include when: Katina's heroic, idealised father is revealed to be a murdered traitor in *Antamosi*; Alex's best friend self-immolates in front of her after being molested by her father in *Only the Brave*; Ari sees transgendered friend Johnny/Toula brutalised by police in *Head On*; Daniel is abducted and tortured in *The Book of Revelation*; and Rhonda looks for her children in *Blessed* only to learn that they have accidentally burned to death. That trauma is a uniting experience across Kokkinos's outsiders foregrounds the vulnerability of the marginalised in confronting and, across the chronology of her oeuvre, increasingly visceral ways: close-ups, slow motion, and exaggerated uses of colour and sound, as noted in later chapters, variously emphasise the physicality of trauma in particular, and the outsider's point-of-view more broadly. To some extent, Kokkinos invites audiences to experience outsider embodiments, to empathise with the outsider's point-of-view by looking with, rather than at the outsider. While Stratton (2017) argues that Australian cinema's preoccupation with outsiders is about 'bring[ing] the outsiders in from the edge', for Kokkinos it is about bringing audiences to that 'edge' and insisting that they see and experience it.

Indeed, the figure of the outsider in Kokkinos's oeuvre functions as a witness to the confronting failures of inclusion, and of hegemonic institutions more broadly, in the Australian cultural landscape, offering a counter-testimony to prevailing discourses of Australian nationhood at the time of these films' release. Certainly at the time of Kokkinos's emergence as a filmmaker, the Australian zeitgeist was marked by a national negotiation of the place of the outsider in Australian society. In 1989, for example – three years before Kokkinos released her first film and the year before she undertook her first filmmaking course – the Australian Federal Government released the *National Agenda for a Multicultural Australia*, which called for a shift away from an official view of Australia as a predominantly white colonial nation[5] and towards multiculturalism as a national policy across cultural, social, and economic sectors (Australian Government 1989).The emphasis in the *National Agenda* was on acknowledging Australia's multicultural diversity largely through a unifying commitment to Australia: immigrants should, former Prime Minister Paul Keating stipulated, 'accept the basic principles of Australian society. These include the Constitution and the rule of law, parliamentary democracy, freedom of speech and religion, English as a national language, equality of the sexes and tolerance' (qtd in Ozdowski 2012). Tom O'Regan (1996: 20, 23) has argued that multiculturalism was effectively offered as a 'new public myth of the people' with the 1989 *National Agenda* providing 'an impetus, albeit in a limited fashion, for cultural diversity to move [. . .] into the mainstream'. But it was a short-lived mainstreaming that was increasingly associated with public unrest: in 1996 the conservative John Howard, who had been critical of multiculturalism (among other sites of difference), was elected prime minister and remained so until 2007 (Tavan 2006). Among his early decisions in office were the abandoning 'of the multicultural portfolio' and the closure of the Office of Multicultural Affairs (Ozdowski 2012; Koleth 2010).[6] One of the effects of the *National Agenda* around multiculturalism and its rejection, of course, is that the 'ethnic' immigrant was discursively negotiated as Australian 'other'.

Nevertheless, at the time the shift in policy represented a key contextual influence to Australian filmmakers, as the film industry was subsidised by the government, and a propitious, albeit brief, moment for broadening and diversifying cultural representations in film. And certainly there were a number of prominent films released in the policy's wake that were set in multicultural milieus, most notably *Death in Brunswick* (dir. John Ruane, 1990), *Strictly Ballroom* (dir. Baz Luhrmann, 1992), and *The Heartbreak Kid* (dir. Michael Jenkins, 1993). French writes:

> When Kokkinos emerged in the 1990s, *Cinema Papers*, amongst others, was heralding a 'New Breed of Ethnic Filmmakers'. [...] Filmmakers like Kokkinos, Alexis Velis and Monica Pellizzari were encouraged to make films that reflected their ethnic backgrounds. Multicultural stories gained greater funding and mainstream exposure, even with non-ethnic filmmakers (for example, Baz Luhrmann's *Strictly Ballroom*, 1992). (French 2013: n.p.)

And perhaps even 'especially' with non-ethnic filmmakers. Certainly the prominent 'multicultural' films released in cinemas in the early 1990s were overwhelmingly directed by non-ethnic and/or male directors, a number of which (as I note further in Chapter 1) told comedic stories about 'caricatured' characters from the perspective of ethnically unmarked, male characters (Callahan 2001). Yet despite these national discourses, and the prominent paradigm of an eventually good-natured acceptance of the 'ethnic other' depicted in much mainstream Australian cinema of the time, Kokkinos's films foreground the often violent and traumatic failures of inclusion in practice, typically through a confronting social realism.[7] Kokkinos, John Conomos (2014: 121) writes, depicts a 'rupture with [...] conservative notions of Australian identity'.

For Kokkinos, this challenge to 'conservative notions of Australian identity' occurs across her oeuvre, but also occurs discursively and extra-textually. As implied earlier, Kokkinos, like her protagonists, is also a multiply marginalised outsider as a lesbian, Greek-Australian director who grew up in a working-class family, which might also go some way to understanding the comparative lack of attention she and her films have received in comparison with her peers. Certainly Kokkinos has described being a Greek-Australian filmmaker in the early 1990s as 'incredibly rare at the time, and in some ways still rare' to the extent that 'to come from an ethnic background, a Greek background, was not only unusual, but fairly unique' (in White and Lambropoulos 2017). But in a national cinema both textually and extra-textually characterised by its emphasis on white, typically heterosexual men (Berry 1999), Kokkinos's ethnicity is by no means her only point of difference to the film industry norms in which she operates.

French, for example, has argued that simply being a female director in Australia constitutes having an 'outsider's view' (paraphrased in Hancock 2014: 5). Indeed, the proportion of female to male directors in Australia is so dire that a national intervention – the AU$3 million 'Gender Matters' initiative by Screen Australia – is currently under way to increase women's participation in key roles, including specifically as directors (Molloy 2016). While women now account for approximately half of all students in Australian film schools, male directors account for almost 85 per cent of all feature films, and have done since the 1970s (Davidson 2015). Such structural bias is reflected in the reception of Australian women filmmakers, too. Consider Aaron Krach's (1999: n.p.) backhanded assertion that 'Anna [sic] Kokkinos is living proof that female filmmakers don't necessarily make "women's films".'

Chris Berry (1999: 35) has further argued that the reception of Kokkinos's first feature, *Head On* (1998), frequently 'pigeonhole[d]' it as 'a gay or ethnic film' and, to some extent, the same can be said of the director herself (French 2012). Certainly discussions frequently draw attention to Kokkinos not simply as a 'director', but specifically as a 'lesbian director' (for example, Lamble 2012: n.p.; Kennerson 1999: 35; Hunn 2000: 113). It is a label Kokkinos has explicitly rejected:

I mean I'm out [...]. And I've been in a relationship for a while now with a woman [...]. But, at the same time, I don't also identify myself as a 'lesbian' filmmaker. I reject that tag. Listen, I am a filmmaker. I have the capacity to represent all kinds of characters on screen and tell a variety of stories with all kinds of characters in a compelling and interesting way for the broadest possible audience. (Kokkinos qtd in Thomas 1999: n.p.)

As with similar debates that have occurred internationally around other lesbian filmmakers, the 'lesbian' descriptor has frequently been feared to delimit a film's potential audience to only those who identify as lesbian or lesbian-friendly, effectively 'ghettoizing' a director's work (Wilton 1995: 13). As Julia Knight (1995: 46) has argued (in relation to the work of Monica Treut), the 'lesbian' descriptor is frustratingly feared to 'deny the broader appeal and, more importantly, the wider relevance of her work'. But while 'lesbian' is often employed as something of a proud acceptance in certain contexts, as with Kokkinos's reception in the queer press, it may also hint at why her films (most of which feature prominent queer characters) have received comparatively little attention. Berry has raised the same spectre:

Some have suggested to me that it is precisely this very marked ethnic and gay combination that has led to critical neglect of [*Head On*]. They have pointed out that since nearly all of Australia's prominent film critics are Anglo and straight, and most of them are male, they could not be expected to grasp a film like *Head On*. (Berry 1999: 35)

Or, perhaps, a director like Kokkinos and her larger body of work.

The book

In this book, I take up the points raised throughout this Introduction to offer a reading of and across Kokkinos's fictional films through the broad focus of tracing the deployment of the outsider as a textual motif. I extend this reading, in the concluding chapter, to consider the extra-textual construction of Kokkinos's fictional oeuvre in interviews, and particularly the framing of it as, as the book's subtitle indicates, an 'oeuvre of outsiders'. In doing this, I pursue a number of organising questions, including:

- How are the protagonists in Kokkinos's fictional films depicted as 'outsiders' and what features characterise the outsider within and across these films?
- What characterises Kokkinos's filmmaking style, in terms of both technical and thematic preoccupations, including (but not limited to) her depictions of the outsider?
- And to what extent can Kokkinos's 'oeuvre of outsiders' support a reading of her as an auteur?

In investigating these framing questions, the book is divided into five chapters organised chronologically around the release dates of her films.

Chapter 1. *Antamosi* and *Only the Brave*: the early films

Chapter 1 examines Kokkinos's early work by looking at her student short *Antamosi* and her short feature *Only the Brave*. In this chapter, I am broadly interested in establishing the features and preoccupations of Kokkinos's developing style, including the stylised social realism and focus on Greek-Australian migrant families in working-class Melbourne for which she is best known. In Chapter 1 I also track the emergence and characteristics of the proto-outsider, emerging first in the final scene of *Antamosi* before its explicit realisation from the first scene of *Only the Brave*. I look particularly at the construction of protagonist Alex as an outsider in terms of class, gender, ethnicity, and sexuality in *Only the Brave*, as well as noting her role as a witness to social injustice and trauma.

Chapter 2. *Head On:* centring the other

Chapters 2–4 each focus on one of Kokkinos's feature films, with Chapter 2 focused on her first feature film, *Head On*. *Head On* was a critical and commercial success; it was widely celebrated as a 'landmark' film in relation to its explicit and unapologetic depiction of queerness in particular, and continues to be exhibited in film festivals around the world almost two decades after its release. This chapter builds on discussions that posit *Head On* (and, for some scholars, *Only the Brave* before it) as the first example(s) of 'New Queer Cinema' in Australia. In doing this, I focus on Kokkinos's increasingly bold focus or 'centring' of an outsider or 'Othered' protagonist, and note the recurrence of the outsider as a witness to social injustice and trauma. I argue that the latter reveals the outsider in Kokkinos's oeuvre as a pretext for a denaturalising appraisal of Australian social and cinematic norms (which, as I argue in Chapter 3, is reinforced in *The Book of Revelation* when its hegemonic protagonist is 'othered'). However, I argue that unlike other social-realist films which tend to favour a didactic tone, Kokkinos's films' emphasis on the traumatised body instead invites an affective, and specifically queer, mode of engagement from audiences, which is emphasised by her refusal to recuperate protagonist Ari into any fixed identity or narrative conclusion.

Chapter 3 (with Sharon Bickle). *The Book of Revelation*: othering the centre

Chapter 3 is focused on Kokkinos's most controversial film, *The Book of Revelation*. In this chapter I, with Sharon Bickle, am interested in the depiction of the film's protagonist Daniel, who, as a successful, white, hetero-masculine man is the only hegemonic protagonist of Kokkinos's oeuvre. It is therefore interesting that he is also the only protagonist that does not witness traumatic social injustice but is instead the victim of it. We argue that Daniel's abduction and torture disorientates him so profoundly that he is forcibly recast as an outsider to his own life – he changes his name and leaves his previous job, house, partner, and profession on his release from capture. Moreover, where *Head On* focused on or 'centred' a marginalised character or 'Other', we argue that *The Book of Revelation* can be read as the reverse: as 'othering' the standard hero of much Australian cinema, namely the white, heterosexual, Anglo-Irish man (Seco 2008). We examine how this occurs through a rewriting of the rape-revenge genre and conclude by exploring a reading of the film as a violent rejection of masculinist Australian film mythologies.

Chapter 4. *Blessed*: an ensemble of outsiders

Chapter 4 focuses on *Blessed*, the release of which marked a return to a critically successful reception for Kokkinos after the comparatively unpopular *The Book of Revelation*. In this chapter I am interested in examining Kokkinos's expanded use of the motifs, style, and preoccupations evident in her previous films. I also note a key shift: specifically, where *Only the Brave*, *Head On*, and *The Book of Revelation* all focus on a single outsider protagonist, most of whom are the sites of intersectional marginalities – ethnicity, class, sexuality, youth – *Blessed* disperses these diversities across an ensemble of outsiders. In doing so, Kokkinos makes explicit her ongoing emphasis on pluralistic depictions of Australian identity and on looking from the margins.

Conclusion: an oeuvre of outsiders – an Australian auteur?

In my concluding chapter, I look briefly at the features across, rather than within, Kokkinos's films. All of her fictional films, for example, are set in contemporary Melbourne, focus on characters who are outsiders, and do so with a strong emphasis on affect and the body within a stylised realism. In this chapter, I query whether these characteristics, among others, are sufficient to support a reading of Kokkinos as an auteur. To this evidence, I also consider extra-textual information and, in particular, Kokkinos's own framing of her films and oeuvre in reviews and interviews in which she regularly draws attention to her celebration of the outsider. In arguing for a reading of Kokkinos as an auteur, I conclude by considering the significance of the claim in the context of Australian cinema more broadly, and particularly Kokkinos's own role as an 'outsider' figure in the industry.

Notes

1   I use 'queer' to denote 'a range of nonstraight expressions' including 'lesbian, and bisexual expressions' but also 'all other potential (and potentially unclassifiable) nonstraight positions' (Doty 1993: xvi).

2   Queer coming-of-age films are overwhelming dominated by male-focused narratives with few focused on the stories of girls and, even at the time of writing, even fewer directed by 'queer women' (Lodge 2018: n.p.).

3   I follow Lisa French (2003: 107) in distinguishing 'short' and 'short feature' as follows: 'Short films are generally defined as films under 60 minutes final running time. As they are not constrained by the need to fill an appropriate time slot, unlike television programs or indeed features which must be within a certain length for exhibition, shorts can be three minutes, or 29, or 42. However, there is a length of short film designated "short feature" that is more well-defined, around the television hour'.

4   Specifically, Kokkinos has directed episodes in the following television programmes: *Eugenie Sandler P.I.* (2000), *Young Lions* (2002), *The Secret Life of Us* (2003–5), *Australia on Trial: Massacre at Myall Creek* (2012), *The Time of Our Lives* (2013), *Seven Types of Ambiguity* (2017), and *Pulse* (2017).

5   Beginning with (but not limited to) the Immigration Restriction Act 1901 until its abolition in 1973, Australia had in place a series of policies that explicitly sought to limit migration to Australia by non-British peoples by 'favouring applicants from certain countries' (Australian Government n.d.). These became known as the 'White Australia Policy'.

6   In many ways, this shift away from multiculturalism is one that has persisted in Australia: 'The last fifteen years have seen a rise in anxiety surrounding

official discourses of multiculturalism, evident both in public debates surrounding the issue, as well as a decrease in the use of the language of multiculturalism itself. Since the late 1990s, Australia has witnessed the diminishing currency of multiculturalism as a national policy priority, largely because of the ascendancy of a conservative politics of Anglo nationalism on the political right (Papastergiadis, 2012). In the popular imagination, the "war on terror" and the politicisation of asylum seekers and refugees have emphasised the divisive nature of cultural difference' (Khan et al. 2013: 27).

7   Though Kokkinos employs different genres and styles within her oeuvre – from social-realist dramas (*Antamosi*), melodramas (*Blessed*), and coming-of-age films (*Only the Brave, Head On*) to a rape-revenge film (*The Book of Revelation*) – she typically favours a stylised social-realist approach. I use 'social realism' to denote a filmmaking style rather than a genre, as it is sometimes used. As a style, social realism crosses genre boundaries – evidenced by its use as a descriptor of much Australian cinema (O'Regan 1996: 97) or of a particular approach to genre, as in 'social-realist coming-of-age films' (Gottschall 2010: 178) – rather than constitutive of a specific genre itself.

1

Antamosi and *Only the Brave*: the early films

Kokkinos wrote and directed *Antamosi* (1991) as a filmmaking student at the VCA and released *Only the Brave* (1994), which she directed and co-wrote with partner Mira Robertson, two years after her 1992 graduation. The latter, her professional debut, premiered at the Melbourne International Film Festival in 1994 and quickly garnered critical attention. The film won the 'Grand Prix for Best Film' at its festival premiere, for example, and later won two awards at the 1994 Australian Film Institute Awards (namely 'Best Short Fiction Film' and 'Best Screenplay in a Non-Feature Film'). For Paul Byrnes (n.d.c) in his curation of the Australian Screen archives, *Only the Brave* was 'clear evidence that a major new voice had arrived in Australian film'. For Kokkinos, who released her first professional film at thirty-six years of age, the career change had been a success and had placed her 'at the forefront of the new directing talent in the country' (Katsigiannis 1998: 6). Moreover, more than two decades later, the film continues to resonate: recently re-released as part of the Melbourne International Film Festival's 2017 celebration of 'Pioneering Women', *Only the Brave* featured alongside the work of other high-profile Australian women directors, including Gillian Armstrong and Tracey Moffatt.

There are important reasons to consider these two films together in this chapter. For one, they are Kokkinos's first films as well as her only non-feature films: *Antamosi* is a 37-minute short, while *Only the Brave* is a 59-minute short feature. For another, they both prefigure the outsider central to Kokkinos's

oeuvre and establish her emerging stylistic and thematic preoccupations. These films also share important contexts having
both been released in the early 1990s, including the comparative
mainstreaming of multiculturalism and queerness in Australia,
the international trend towards social realism, and the Australian
cycle of women-centred films. To very briefly flag these contexts:
in the late 1980s and 1990s, Australian cinema was characterised
by dual shifts towards internationalisation and co-productions on
the one hand, as the imperatives of a cash-strapped national film
industry looking for opportunities for commercial collaboration,
and towards more plural representations of the local and national
on the other hand (O'Regan 2001). The latter was fuelled by
shifts in government policy, most notably the 1989 *National
Agenda for a Multicultural Australia*, as well as by broader social
and cultural shifts, including around more inclusive attitudes
towards queerness. Indeed, the early 1990s saw the increasing
institutionalisation of gay and lesbian studies in universities;
the increasing popularity of 'queer' as an umbrella term for non-
heteronormative sexualities (Jagose 1996); the emergence of
New Queer Cinema (which I take up further in the following
chapter); and the emergence of gays (and, to a lesser extent,
lesbians) in mainstream popular culture in Western industrialised
nations. Deborah Hunn has described this as the 'queer moment':

> In Australia the queer moment has coincided resonantly
> with a shift in more general debates about what constitutes
> Australian identity. [...] [In the] 1980s and 1990s, 'the
> official story of Australian identity was built around the
> idea of a multicultural, cosmopolitan and tolerant society
> embracing and invigorated by change', a move which led
> to a degree of inclusiveness towards gays and lesbians and
> some recognition of sexual identity as a legitimate area
> of concern in the dialogue that was reshaping national
> identity. (Hunn 2000: 113, quoting Reynolds 1999: 58–9)

These shifts are, to different extents, reflected in the multicultural
and queer cycles of Australian cinema at the time. Certainly films
featuring multicultural characters and milieus were entering the

Australian cinematic mainstream in increasing numbers in the early 1990s (Collins 2009). Indeed, as noted in the Introduction, a number of successful comedies focused on multicultural milieus were released, most notably *Death in Brunswick* (1990), *The Heartbreak Kid* (1993), and perhaps most influentially, *Strictly Ballroom* (1992).[1] *Strictly Ballroom* offers affable, though often 'caricatured' representations of Spaniards – and specifically the 'tourist cliché of the Andalusian gypsy' – who stand in contrast to comedically dysfunctional 'suburban white Australians' (Callahan 2001: 97). The narrative eventually moves towards a good-natured acceptance of the 'ethnic other', which is symbolised by a crowd clapping on the Spanish-influenced new dance steps of ethnically unmarked protagonist Scott (Paul Mercurio) and ethnically marked love interest Fran (Tara Morice) at a dance competition (O'Regan 1996). But for James Bennett, this neatly packaged and highly 'managed' representation of ethnicity reflects a 'good multiculturalism', in which the audience are invited to 'extend, through tolerance, the boundaries of Australian identity to the Other' (2007: 61). While Bennett's (2007) 'good multicultural-ism' functions to mask the reality of the hegemonic, it perhaps also reveals the fraught tension between the conflicting trends within the industry at the time, namely of both a nostalgic return to nationalism as well as an 'open-ness' to change (Craven 2001: 2).

This negotiation over what could be represented in Australian cinema at the time was also occurring around sexuality. Indeed, queer characters also began to emerge in the Australian cinematic mainstream in the mid 1990s, with the release of explicitly queer films like *The Adventures of Priscilla, Queen of the Desert* (1994), *The Sum of Us* (1994), and *Love and Other Catastrophes* (1996), and preceded by implicitly queer films like *Muriel's Wedding* (1994). According to Hunn (2005: 38), these films heralded the so-called 'explosion of queer Australian films in the 1990s'. Certainly they collectively mark a very significant shift towards explicit and non-punitive representations of queerness in mainstream Australian cinema. Deb Verhoeven (1997: 25) has argued that before this time the representation of 'queer characters in

Australian films ha[d] [. . .] been almost entirely and quite literally "in the closet". Nevertheless, the most prominent films of this first wave of Australian queer cinema – namely *Priscilla* and *The Sum of Us*, which both garnered significant national attention – have been widely criticised for their problematic representations. *Priscilla* (1994), for example, has been criticised for emphatically misogynistic and racist depictions of women, lesbian, and Asian characters (Brooks 1999; Rustin 2001; Kunze 2013), while *The Sum of Us* has been criticised for its heterosexism and misogyny (Berry 1995). These films, again all comedies,[2] nonetheless represent a prominent precedent – as the ostensibly 'wholesome representations of lesbians and gays that Australia's multicultural context had [. . .] tried to nurture' (Jennings and Lominé 2004: 147) – and are key counterpoints to the confronting social-realist representations of queers and queerness that Kokkinos offers in *Only the Brave*, *Head On*, and *Blessed*.

Indeed, another context that Kokkinos's early films reflect is the international trend towards social realism in the early 1990s. Though Kokkinos employs different genres and styles within her oeuvre – from social-realist dramas (*Antamosi*), melodramas (*Blessed*), and coming-of-age films (*Only the Brave*, *Head On*) to a rape-revenge film (*The Book of Revelation*) – she typically favours a stylised realist approach. Social-realist films are most associated with uncompromising depictions of social injustice and are typically focused on marginalised characters in working-class milieus: 'characters who usually figure as background presences in the generic mainstream, who are marginalised by virtue of their social status and/or ethnic identity' (Hallam and Marshment 2000: 190; see also Dermody and Jacka 1988a). Both the broader Australian and international cinematic contexts were strongly reflecting social realism at the time of Kokkinos's emergence with a 'new and global cycle of realism in Western cinema' taking shape in the 1990s (Jorgensen 2005: 147). This contemporary social realism has inevitably been employed in different ways in different cinemas, but is broadly marked by an interest in the 'politics of representation' (Hallam and Marshment 2000: 190) that is typically enunciated through masculine protagonists. The latter is particularly true of the historically androcentric Australian cinema (Jorgensen 2005), although there were a 'handful' of Australian social-realist films focused on women in the 1980s and 1990s (Hancock 2014: 5). Grady Hancock (2014) identifies *Fran* (1985), *Sweetie* (1989), and *Radiance* (1998), all directed by women, as emblematic of this 'handful' of gynocentric Australian social-realist films of the period. To these, we can add Kokkinos's *Antamosi* and *Only the Brave*, both of which are focused on female protagonists (and in the former, on three generations of women).

There was also a broader cycle of women-centred films in Australia during the same period, which alongside *Sweetie* included films like Jackie McKimmie's *Waiting* (1991), Gillian Armstrong's *Last Days of Chez Nous* (1992), and Susan Lambert's *Talk* (1994). Though diverse in preoccupations, these films tended to eschew a focus on 'heterosexual romance as a goal of the plot' and instead foreground the 'relations between women' (O'Regan 1995: n.p.). Lizzie Francke (1993: 19) has described these (alongside key New Zealand films) as an 'Australasian new female wave', although few of these films gained attention comparable to their cultural significance at the time.[3] Among them, Campion is internationally well-known for her ongoing emphasis on the stories of strong, complex, female characters and was arguably the most prominent figure in the shift in Australian cinema of the late 1980s and 1990s towards women-centred texts (French 2007; Hancock 2014: 5), a trend to which both *Antamosi* and *Only the Brave* can be seen as contributing. Interestingly, Kokkinos has cited Campion as an early influence: 'there was no doubt that for me, particularly in that period, Jane Campion's work was very inspirational because, again, another very strong woman director was emerging [...] [T]hat was a terrific impetus' (qtd in Barber 1998: 5).

It was within these broad and overlapping contexts that Kokkinos emerged in Australian cinema in the early 1990s. In this chapter, then, I am broadly interested in establishing the features and preoccupations of Kokkinos's developing style, including the social-realist focus on Greek-Australian migrant families in working-class Melbourne for which she is best known. I also track the emergence and characteristics of the proto-outsider, emerging first in the final scene of *Antamosi* before its partial realisation from the first scene of *Only the Brave*. As such, I am particularly interested in the construction of protagonists Katina in *Antamosi* and Alex in *Only the Brave*, including in terms of class, gender, ethnicity, and sexuality. Together, these early films reveal important insights into Kokkinos's emerging style as she progresses from film student to filmmaker.

Antamosi

Written, edited, and directed by Kokkinos, *Antamosi* is a short black-and-white film set in Melbourne that depicts the relationship between three generations of women in a Greek-Australian family. With *Antamosi* Kokkinos begins her 'filmic preoccupation with exploring Greek-Australian migrant life in Melbourne' (French 2013: n.p.). And as with other Australian filmmakers of the period interested in '"looking" and representing onscreen the experience of parents who travelled and settled in Australia', the '"looking" is done through the eyes of children' (Tuccio 2008: 18–19). In this instance, the film is told from the perspective of the youngest daughter, seven-year-old Sophia (played by Xaris Miller, but whose adult-self voice-over is performed by Helen Trenos), and focuses on the fraught relationship between her mother Katina (played by Phillippa Adgemis) and her namesake grandmother Sophia (played by Stella Stefanidis), who is visiting from Greece. Grandmother Sophia is in many ways the obvious 'outsider' both to Australia and to her daughter, from whom she is estranged. But it is Greek immigrant Katina who is the film's protagonist and, as I argue later in this section, the first outsider of Kokkinos's oeuvre, though by no means as emphatic an outsider as the protagonists in her later films.

The film itself is focused on the mother–daughter dyad – first, Katina and her mother Sophia, and later Katina and her daughter

Sophia – which is refracted through the lens of the working-class, Greek-Australian family. While I return to the film's foregrounding of constructions of motherhood later in this section, the cultural differences between Greece and Australia are initially flagged through clothing. Grandma Sophia arrives in a simple, dark dress with a dark scarf – stereotypical peasant garb reflective of the elderly woman's origins in a poor, rural village – wrapped around her grey hair. Her relatives (Katina and husband Basili, alongside Sophia and older sister Crystalos) are all dressed in conservative but modern clothes, contrasting the old and (negotiated) new worlds of the migrant. The 'new' world is symbolised by Madge (played by Maureen Hartley), a white Australian hairdresser for whom Katina briefly works – although notably by whom she is never paid – and the only female character outside the family. Madge talks in 'ocker', or stereotypically vernacular ways.[4] On Katina's first day of work, for instance, Madge pours them both a drink saying: 'Cheers luv, down the hatch.' Madge then notes, 'You know, 'Tina, you're not a bad looker really. You should do something with yourself'. Madge proceeds to put a short, blonde wig on Katina, before telling her she now looks like 'a doll'. In doing so, Madge makes explicit the hegemonic Australian ideal, first by anglicising Katina's name (to Tina), and second by reconstructing her in the image of a white woman. Katina's differences can be 'tolerated' by the white Australian – in a scene demonstrative of Bennett's (2007: 61) notion of 'good multiculturalism' – but are nevertheless incongruent with the hegemonic ideal.

In contrast, Katina's Greek origins are revealed through the family's alternation between English and Greek, through flashbacks to rural Greece, and by drawing on 'tropes used to signify Greekness in earlier Australian cinema, where it is repeatedly identified with Greek folk music and folk dancing, with weddings, with oppression (both political and cultural)' (Freiberg and Damousi 2003: 219). Though there is no folk dancing in *Antamosi* (as there is in *Head On*), the film nevertheless begins and ends with Greek folk music, while grandmother Sophia notes the importance of marriage (and particularly of daughters securing marriages to financially prosperous men). Numerous oppressions are also touched upon: the Military Junta in Greece when Katina was growing up, the oppressions of the stereotypically patriarchal Greek family on women, and the oppressions of the working-class that Basili's strike unsuccessfully attempts to challenge. Like *The Heartbreak Kid* (1993), then, *Antamosi* 'complicates the issue of ethnicity by introducing class differences' (Freiberg and Damousi 2003: 218), as do *Only the Brave*, *Head On*, and *Blessed*, and is an early indicator of Kokkinos's emerging interest in intersectional outsiders. In *Antamosi*, Katina embodies these overlapping sites of difference until her breakdown at the film's end.

Kokkinos signals her approach to these issues through the film's title – 'antamosi', an English translation of the Greek word αντάμωση meaning 'meeting again' or, more broadly, 'coming together'. The title can be read as the re-meeting or 'coming together' of migrants in a new country. But it also functions to introduce the central relationship of the film, as daughter Sophia notes in her voice-over at the film's start: 'Grandma's visit – Mum hadn't seen Grandma for eighteen years.' The women are, quite literally, meeting again after a long absence. But their reunion is by no means a warm one. The women's fraught relationship is initially depicted through the absence of intimacy which, given that most of the film is set in the intimate sphere of the family home, sets familial relationships up as the key site of drama in the film. Indeed, while the rest of the family all hug the older woman on her airport arrival, Katina stands away from her, staring in silence, and eventually extends a hand to her mother's arm in a demonstration of their distance, literally holding her 'at arm's length'. Katina's hostility to her mother is made more explicit – though it is still unexplained at this point – in later scenes where, for example, her daughters cook grandmother Sophia a surprise breakfast but Katina takes the unfinished plate away from her mother and scolds her daughters for wasting food.

Where father Basili is depicted as playful and irresponsible, and grandmother Sophia as warm and compassionate with her grand-daughters (though wary of her daughter), Katina is depicted as an inexplicable antagonist to her mother and a disciplinarian to her children. This construction of Katina both foregrounds and problematises key constructions of motherhood. The 'good' mother, as identified by Terry Arendell (1999: 3), is a white, married, heterosexual woman who is both financially dependent upon her husband and solely occupied with the task of mothering, though Susan Goodwin and Kate Huppatz (2010: 2–3) expand on this to note that there are numerous 'variations on' this theme, such as the 'good working mother' or the 'good mother on welfare'. Key, then, is that the good mother is 'self-sacrificing, devoted and passive' and her emphasis is on nurturing her family – the 'family unit' being the 'foundation of society' and the site through which mothers 'socialise girls to be mothers' (Pascoe 1998: 6, 12). Moreover, this focus must also fulfil her emotionally. A good mother is thus a happy one, whereas 'an unhappy mother is a failed mother' (Johnston and Swanson 2003: 23).

But Katina is shown as unhappy for most of the film, outside of one brief scene. In fact, Katina is constrained both within and by family in a clear demonstration of the limits of notions of the good mother. This plays out in relation to space, for as French (2012: 66) notes, *Antamosi* 'establishes [Kokkinos's] exposition of psychological landscapes, the inside of her characters'. Most of the film takes place in the run-down family home – in its rooms and, to a lesser extent, backyard – which is depicted, for Katina, as a site of restriction and containment. In the home, shots are tightly, even claustrophobically framed with Katina usually stonily faced serving others: ironing, mending socks, clearing away dishes. The only moment Katina is shown relaxed, chatting, and joking warmly is when she is outside the home and away from the family. The house is also gendered, implicating the role of gender inequality, among other marginalisations, in her unhappiness: when Basili has a group of men over discussing the strike, Katina only enters the space to serve the men before leaving the room and closing the doors behind her, separating the male and female spaces of the home. Katina's containment by the family plays out in relation to her husband in more direct ways, too. For example,

Katina has to ask her husband for money, even as his role as breadwinner is undermined (he is fired after going on strike). He tells her one night, after returning home unemployed and drunk, that she is his 'good little wife', because she 'mends socks', 'cooks and cleans'. That she remains silent and downcast throughout his short monologue positions her, at least in this moment, as the stereotypically obedient Greek wife and mother typical of much Australian cinema (Freiberg and Damousi 2003). But it is a role with which she is struggling amid cultural, financial, and familial pressures that are brought together and intensified by the arrival of her own mother and their long-unresolved issues.

The cause of Katina's hostility to her mother is eventually revealed to centre around her deceased father. Katina remembers him as a hero who died fighting for the Greek resistance, whom she has mythologised in oft-told bedtime stories to her youngest daughter. Katina narrates:

> Well your grandpa was a tall, handsome man. He had a long moustache that he used to twirl with his fingers. I remember when he stood at our house waving us goodbye. He was going to the mountains to fight the fascists. They wanted to take what little we had away from us. Your grandpa was fighting for a new Greece. To have enough to eat. To have work. For people to be equal. That's why he was a communist.

Here he is the idealised hero in his daughter's familial fairy-tale, a narrative around which she has built her life. In her discussion of the work of Sylvia Plath, Susan Schwartz (2017: 218) has discussed this as the 'dead father effect' on a daughter, where the daughter remains 'shackled to the absent and dead connection'. In *Antamosi*, we might extend this to Katina being 'shackled' to the hetero-patriarchal ideologies that he represented, too. Certainly Katina is traumatised when her mother offers a conflicting account of her father in the penultimate scene in the film, which effectively severs Katina's anchor to her own life and results in her psychotic break. In an earlier conversation that triggers the revelation, grandmother Sophia tells Katina that she is selling the family home in rural Greece to move to the city. Katina responds with 'My father's house? [. . .] You were never proud of what he did [. . .] You embarrass me.' That Katina dismisses her mother and considers the house her deceased father's indicates not only her complicity in patriarchy, but equally her inability to see herself: she is, after all, living a life not dissimilar to the subservient role of Greek wife and mother that her own mother once occupied. Indeed, Kokkinos's stylised framing emphasises a reading of Katina and her mother as reflections or doubles – a visual enactment of the mother–daughter dyad – through mirroring (see Figure 1.1) and identical poses (see Figure 1.2).

Alongside the symbolic visuals, Kokkinos further emphasises their role as doubles through their near-identical circumstances, despite the different countries in which they live: both women are mothers to two daughters and wife to a husband who is unsuccessfully engaged in political action. For grandmother Sophia, her husband was engaged in the Greek resistance to fight for better conditions, but died a traitor to the cause. For Katina, her husband is engaged in a strike to fight for better conditions, but is instead fired. Where Katina criticises her husband for his role in

Figure 1.1 Katina and Sophia in mirrored poses in *Antamosi*

Figure 1.2 Katina and Sophia in identical poses in *Antamosi*

the strike, Basili counters that his daughters will 'think I'm a hero', just as Katina views her own deceased father at the expense of her relationship with her mother.

In doing so, Kokkinos problematises the mother-blaming trope prevalent in Australian cinema (among many other sites around the world), which is part of broader patriarchal discourses of the 'good' (and 'bad') mother flagged earlier (Reimer and Sahagian 2015). Core to this trope is the assumption that the mother is responsible both for any conflict between her and her child as well as for all of her 'child's problems' (Pascoe 1998: 22). In *Antamosi*, the trope is initially implied through protagonist Katina's barely veiled hostility to her mother on her airport arrival; Katina clearly blames her mother for some significant, mysterious wrongdoing, and the audience is invited to do so, too, viewing her as a suspicious site of motherhood. However, Katina's mother-blaming is depicted as increasingly unreasonable. As the film progresses, Katina's hostility escalates in inexplicable ways – from removing food from her mother's unfinished plate to excluding her from outings – which is contrasted to grandmother

Sophia's wary but otherwise empathetic behaviour. Through this contrast, which occupies much of the film, Kokkinos invites audiences to call into question Katina's 'blaming' of her mother, before eventually revealing it as the undeserved result of a misunderstanding: grandmother Sophia does not also hero-worship Katina's dead father, because he was never a hero.

One of the implications of the mother-blaming trope is that if the mother is responsible for her child's problems then, as Caroline Pascoe (1998: 22) points out, 'the daughter' is subsumed 'into the role of victim, without control of her life'. The mother-blaming trope and broader discourses of the 'good' mother thus socialise the daughter into the same passive, subservient role of hegemonic motherhood. As flagged through Kokkinos's symbolic representation of Katina and grandmother Sophia as 'doubles' or 'mirror images', then, the daughter becomes the mother who socialises the daughter and so on. Hetero-patriarchal discourses are not a finite removal of a daughter's or mother's agency, but a continuing one that expands into each future generation as girls are brought up within them, the film suggests. The result is that when her tether to her father's narrative is challenged, Katina has no independent sense of self on which to rely; she is instead traumatised and experiences a break with reality.

Indeed, Katina's breakdown is triggered in the penultimate scene of the film when grandmother Sophia reveals: 'You thought he was so wonderful. Eyes only for your father. Your father was a traitor, killed by his comrades.' Katina is horrified and tells her mother to 'Get out!' Indeed, they are the last words she speaks to her mother who returns to Greece the following morning. Her mother's revelation nevertheless triggers a childhood memory of Katina coming across a group of adults standing over her father's dead body, as if confirming her mother's disclosure. In the final scene of the film, which takes place the following morning, Katina breaks down. When daughter Sophia is bumped and spills her drink, Katina roughly undresses her and forces the naked child to stand in the rain in the backyard. As Basili slowly resolves the situation, Katina appears distant and dazed, before mumbling to herself, 'Whichever way I turn . . .', in an apparent psychotic break.

The line is the last Katina speaks in the film before wandering the house in distress as the rest of the family returns grandmother Sophia to the airport. Though not referenced in the film, the line recalls Walt Whitman's 'Out of the Cradle Endlessly Rocking'. The despairing poem about mortality notes an adult whose grief for a lost love has made them child-like again as they ask, 'Whichever way I turn, O I think you could give me my mate back again, if you only would' (Whitman [1885] 1991: 75). Certainly Katina is re-grieving her father, this time her child-like misconception of him and its foundational role in her own sense of self that has now given way. In problematising the deceased patriarch, Kokkinos also calls into question the active patriarchy of Katina and her own family and its impact on her constrained self-identity and mental health. French (2013: n.p.) notes that with *Antamosi* Kokkinos begins a preoccupation that is 'central to her oeuvre, including an interest in female perspectives, trauma, identity, working-class life, and parental influence on relationships'. These interests converge in the film's final shots.

The film concludes with Katina's slow-motion search through the now empty house, first in the absent room recently occupied by her mother, and then holding the gifts her mother brought with her: Katina's dead father's ring and a cross necklace from her mother. The objects are symbols of Katina's estrangement from her absent parents: one deceased, one rejected, but both newly 're-met' apropos the film's title. The final image of the film is a mid-shot of Katina who has transitioned from brightly lit rooms to a dark, dimly lit room. Katina is framed on the left of the image, indicating her unbalanced and gloomy state. In slow motion she runs a hand through her hair with the final image of her hand resting over her heart. The image is of pained estrangement from her family (whom she has just abused and rejected), from her past (which she has misremembered), and from her own sense of (fractured) self. Katina is, in this moment, untethered – an outsider to her own life. The shot is both visceral and affecting:

its slow motion and tight framing encourage an intimate empathy with her distressed estrangement that is externalised through the suddenly dark and unrecognisable mise en scène. These emphases on visceral depictions and psychologically reflective mise en scène are the first examples of Kokkinos's 'dynamic, kinetic and visceral style' (French 2013: n.p.), which increasingly characterises her later films.

Though the film's organisation, indicated by its title, around 'coming together' or 'meeting again' is not realised in the mother–daughter dyad of Katina and grandmother Sophia – or at least, while the women certainly 're-meet', there is no reconciliation – it is realised in the mother–daughter dyad of Katina and daughter Sophia. Over the final image of Katina, the film concludes with daughter Sophia's adult voice-over:

> I was on my way to Greece when Grandma died. Mum gave me the money for the fare. 'You go, you're her namesake,' she said. On the morning of the funeral, the heavens opened up and it poured. As I walked in the procession I kept a space for Mum, just beside me.

Grandmother Sophia's death, like her departure from Australia, are both marked by pouring rain; they are watershed moments for the women in the family. But where her departure showed Katina breaking down, her death shows daughter Sophia picking up the pieces and actively bridging the gap between cultures, countries, and generations. As the VCA's description of the film on YouTube emphasises, the initial 'bitter embrace between mother and daughter [on her arrival] is observed by Katina's own daughter, Sophia, who must play her own role in' these characters' 'estrangement'. Importantly, Sophia rejects discourses of the 'good' or 'bad' mother, or its enunciation through the mother-blaming trope; she goes to her grandmother, and at the same time keeps a 'space' for her mother beside her. Neither are blamed and both are accepted as they are. In this sense, Sophia offers the symbolic 're-meeting' or 'coming together' of her mother and grandmother, with the film concluding, as with all of Kokkinos's films, with a sense of ambiguous optimism via the outsider (in this case, Katina facilitating Sophia's trip to Greece).

But where the prototypical outsider emerges in *Antamosi*'s final scene, the outsider is much more explicitly realised over the course of Kokkinos's second film, *Only the Brave*.

Only the Brave

Only the Brave (1994) is a 59-minute short feature directed and, with Mira Robertson, co-written by Kokkinos. The film was funded by the now defunct Women's Program of the Australian Film Commission (AFI) and the Independent Filmmaker's Fund (IFF) of Film Victoria. While the AFI's Women's Program was designed to bring more Australian women into filmmaking, the IFF had 'the express purpose of funding shorts as a training ground for feature film-making' with the 'intention' being for 'funded films to be more ambitious in scope than a student short, but not as complex as a feature' (French 2003: 109). Certainly the longer format of *Only the Brave* allowed Kokkinos to build and extend upon many of the foci established in *Antamosi*, among them the emergence of the outsider.

Set in the outer western suburbs of Melbourne, *Only the Brave* is a social-realist coming-of-age film that focuses on working-class, queer, Greek-Australian teen Alex (played by Elena Mendalis), who lives with her white Australian father and fantasises about the return of her Greek-Australian mother, who left when Alex was a child. Alex is exploring a same-sex attraction to her teacher Kate (played by Maude Davey) and shares an intense and fraught friendship with troubled school-friend Vicki (played by Dora Kaskanis). Where Alex is a capable and applied student, Vicki is angry, disinterested, and self-destructive. Both girls are rebellious and dream of escaping to Sydney which is where Alex hopes to find her mother and Vicki hopes to begin a singing career. It is revealed late in the film that Vicki is being sexually abused by her father and, traumatised when Alex finds out, she sets alight to herself burning to death with Alex helpless to stop it. The film concludes with Alex leaving town on foot.

The coming-of-age or rite-of-passage film, organised as it is around one or a small group of youth protagonists and their symbolic transition to adulthood, has been a staple of Australian cinema since the late-1960s revival. Jonathan Raynor (2000: 142–3, 145) writes of the genre that the 'protagonist undergoing fundamental formative and traumatic experience, travelling and questing within a country supposedly his own but over which he can exert little control, emerges as a key characteristic of Australian film narratives' in the 1970s and 1980s, with a 'particular emphasis on female adolescence' emerging in the late 1980s and 1990s. Social realism sites this narrative within a working-class milieu and embodied by a socially marginalised protagonist. At the heart of the social-realist coming-of-age film, then, is often an outsider who, through the 'formative' and 'traumatic' experiences they encounter over the course of the film, comes to terms with their emerging independence in an unjust socio-cultural environment.

Alex is established as a social outsider in the first scene of the film, as the ostensible leader of a gang of four Greek-Australian, working-class girls focused on Alex and best friend Vicki, alongside Maria (played by Helen Athanasiadis) and Sylvie (played by Tina Zerella). The film begins at night with the four girls huddled around a lit match before setting alight to bushland. For Whitney Monaghan (2017a: n.p.), they are 'wild girls [...] the kinds of girls that sneak out at night to cause trouble'. Certainly the girls exist on the social margins as rebellious Greek-Australian teenagers in a bleak, working-class environment. Their 'wildness' is reinforced in high-school English class in the following scene. Alex recites a passage from William Golding's (1954) novel *The Lord of the Flies*, which offers a famously dystopian vision of youth at the extremes of marginalisation (literally separated from society as island outcasts). In *Only the Brave* its reference introduces the theme of adolescence as a dangerous, volatile state of liminality that not all of them will survive. The liminality of adolescence is a common theme among coming-of-age films, of course, with their emphasis on the transition between childhood and adulthood. However, as Monaghan writes:

> *Only the Brave* engages with this idea of liminality, but it is not about the possibility of youth. This film gives a sense of being caught in a liminal space between worlds, or of being pulled in multiple directions at once. [...] [Alex] is caught between childhood and adulthood; between her love of literature and her rebellious girl gang; between her Greek heritage and her suburban Australian location; between her queer feelings and the expectation to conform to heterosexuality. [...] Kokkinos replaces the nostalgia of the coming-of-age film with menace, drawing attention to the instability and danger of adolescence by ruminating on fires and the girls who light them. (Monaghan 2017a: n.p.)

This liminality of adolescence is emphasised through muted blue (Monaghan 2017a), black, and grey tones and is sited in specific spaces: night-time scenes of misadventure, the train track, the train yard, an abandoned shack. These spaces – extensions of Kokkinos's 'exposition of psychological landscapes' (French 2012: 66) – are marginalised – unoccupied, run-down, and on the outskirts of town traversed by, as the film's title suggests, 'only the brave'. Though the train tracks in particular hint at the transitional nature of adolescence, Alex and Vicki sit in abandoned train carriages, suggesting their 'stuck-ness' rather than directional potential: here adolescence threatens to be an endless liminality. This threat is reinforced through the film's soundscape. Rather than the up-beat pop soundtrack of most coming-of-age films (Henderson 2007: 262), Kokkinos draws on discordant and eerie tones that are interspersed with background sounds of nearby industry.

Adolescent liminality is also associated, as Monaghan (2017a) noted above, with fire. Richard Dyer with Julianne Pidduck (2003: 280) note that the 'film begins and ends ablaze'. But there are many more fires, too: aside from the girls' arson in the first scene and Vicki's eventual self-immolation, there are also multiple campfires, a fireplace, and Vicki's off-screen arson of the school library – the latter the symbolic antithesis to the protagonist's 'awakening knowledge' in the genre (Caputo 1993). Indeed, fire is an important symbol throughout the film, though it is employed in different ways. For Alex, fire is associated with her queer desire. But fire also symbolises the girls' obverse journeys, and particularly Vicki's increasing volatility and danger. I discuss these separately.

Alex is the first of several queer youth protagonists in Kokkinos's oeuvre (alongside Ari in *Head On* and Roo in *Blessed*), with her queer desire linked to fire several times in the film. And, like her outsider status, Alex's queerness is also evident from the first scene of the film when the girls set alight bushland. The girls are initially silhouetted against the blaze, before Maria and Sylvia run off leaving Alex and Vicki. Vicki dances in front of the fire – first in a slow-motion close-up, running her fingers through her hair in what Monaghan (2017a: n.p.) describes as 'an almost erotic movement', and then in a mid-shot – while Alex is shown watching and smiling. Monaghan (2017a: n.p.) argues, 'This is very clearly a queer point of view and the first glimpse of Alex's desiring gaze.' It also immediately offers a queer orientation to the film, inviting viewers into a queer, outsider gaze. However, Alex's queer desire is made more explicit later in the film with Kate and through increasingly contained depictions of fire.

Alex and Kate share a clear admiration of each other throughout the film that develops a tentatively flirtatious undertone when Kate invites Alex to a poetry reading and the two end up at the teacher's house after the event. The event is framed as queer: it occurs after Kate has lent Alex a book of queer erotica (Anaïs Nin's *Little Birds*), while the female poet (played by Karen Hadfield) reads a poem by lesbian Australian poet Pam Brown. The two sit across a softly lit table and, after the event, sit in front of a fireplace in the living room of Kate's house. The two discuss each other's writing and stroke each other's hair in mise en scène that plays on conventional signifiers of romance (McWilliam 2017a; Harris 2000). Unlike the run-down, often abandoned spaces Alex spends much of the film in, which are often depicted in cool tones, Kate's living room is stylish, middle-class, and shot in the warm orange and red tones of fire. But this fire occurs in a fireplace: unlike the wild blaze that began the film, here it connotes romance and emergent control of sexual maturity, rather than volatility and imminent danger.

Later in the evening, Kate and Alex face each other in a bedroom doorway, a framing device that marks the boundaries of the intimate space of the bedroom and the sexual potential it heralds. While the two lean in to each other kissing briefly, Kate pulls away and the moment ends. Though no further intimacy occurs between the two, queer desire has nevertheless been made evident. That the moment occurs between a student and a teacher is not insignificant, of course. The student–teacher trope has a long history in lesbian cinema from *Mädchen in Uniform* (1931), which is set in a German boarding school and is 'considered the *Urtext* of the schoolgirl genre, a staple of lesbian film' (Mennel 2012: 6), through to more recent films like *Loving Annabelle* (2006) and *Cracks* (2009), which are also set in boarding schools, and *Bloomington* (2010), which extends the trope into an American college setting. In some ways, *Only the Brave* transposes this trope, which is typically set in privileged European or American settings, into a working-class Australian setting. The trope is not unique to lesbian cinema, however; the student–teacher relationship is a common feature of the coming-of-age genre more broadly, 'given that a coming-of-age theme is typically about awakening knowledge of the world' (Caputo 1993: 16). Thus, Alex and Kate's book sharing, poetry reading, and roles as student and teacher – framed as they are within Alex's queer desire – all emphasise the significance of queerness to Alex's coming of age. They do not do so in ways typical of queer coming-of-age films, however.

At the time of its release, *Only the Brave* was not just unusual in eschewing the romanticism of other coming-of-age films (French 2014); it was also unique in focusing on a queer girl in the coming-of-age genre. Indeed, *Only the Brave* was arguably the first queer coming-of-age film in Australia, with the first cycle only emerging in the 2000s[5] with the release of films like *Tan Lines* (2006), *Newcastle* (2008), and, later, *Monster Pies* (2013).[6] *Only the Brave* was also one of, if not 'the' first coming-of-age film internationally to focus on a queer girl. As Glenn Dunks (2015: 27) notes, *Only the Brave* 'was quite unlike its contemporaries by foregrounding [. . .] a queer female voice'. Internationally, queer coming-of-age films emerged in the USA, Britain, and Western Europe in the 1990s. Queer coming-of-age films typically focus on male protagonists, such as in *Get Real* (1998) and *Edge of Seventeen* (1998), undergoing 'all those firsts' for which the genre is known: 'first crush, first date, first kiss, first love, first grope, first time getting drunk, losing your virginity' (Kitson 2008: 30). In queer coming-of-age films, however, those 'firsts' typically occur against a specifically homophobic background, whether symbolised by peers, family, or the school. Though appearing in fewer numbers, queer coming-of-age films with female protagonists also emerged in the mid to late 1990s, most notably with American films *The Incredibly True Adventure of Two Girls in Love* (1995) and *All Over Me* (1997), and the Swedish film *Show Me Love* (1998). Two decades later, the coming-of-age genre is now 'the dominant model of young lesbian representation in world cinema' (Beirne 2012: 259).

Queer coming-of-age films in the 1990s were among the first films to consistently offer sympathetic portrayals of queer youth: 'positive, pro-gay, upbeat' films that reassure audiences that it is 'ok to be gay' in 'repressive and homophobic culture[s]' (Bronski 2000: 26). Perhaps unsurprisingly, then, queer coming-of-age films have also tended to depict queerness in particular ways. While the 'formation' of an independent 'identity' is typical to the genre more broadly, in queer coming-of-age films protagonists usually claim a specifically gay or lesbian identity which is revealed through the protagonist's 'coming out'[7] late in the film (Padva 2004: 355; Bronski 2000). Monaghan (2010: 59) describes this as the 'trope of "coming out as coming of age"'. There is thus a frequent emphasis in queer coming-of-age films of the period of transitioning from one identity (heterosexual) to another (gay or lesbian). Padva writes that many queer teen films

> in the 1990s and 2000s are largely based on the presumed distinction, perhaps even an essentialist dichotomy, between straight and gay sexualities, and presuppose that one should realize what one is to live one's true sexual identity. Characters reflect little sexual fluidity unless they are in transition from one sexual identity to another. And, like their youthful viewers, are often seen as confused queer adolescents. (Padva 2014: 98)

This transition between defined sexualities is evident in most Australian queer coming-of-age films, too.[8] In stark contrast, in *Only the Brave* Alex is not confused or anxious about her sexuality. She also never explicitly self-identifies in any particular way and never 'comes out'. In fact, Alex never refers to her sexuality at all. She is shown arm-in-arm with a male date in one scene (though the two later split) and pursuing her female teacher in a later scene, and both with the same calm self-assuredness. In refusing to depict her sexuality in any fixed way, 'Kokkinos is oblique' about sexuality in the film with Alex depicted as '"queer" rather than lesbian' (Dyer with Pidduck 2003: 281).

But her queerness also completes her transition into a more explicit outsider, which is emphasised when she is literally punished for it in the scene immediately following her night with Kate. Vicki, jealous that Alex chose time with Kate over time with her, tells Tammy (played by Peta Bray), who is the leader of the rival girl gang at school, about the queer date; Tammy then attacks Alex in the school bathroom for being a 'fucking lezzo'. Notably, it is the 'only time' in the film that Alex's queerness 'is explicitly mentioned' (Monaghan 2017a: n.p.). The scene is consistent with most queer coming-of-age films which feature a queer protagonist negotiating a hostile homophobic environment (Padva 2014; McWilliam 2017b), reinforcing both the heteronormativity of space and of coming of age more broadly. It also represents Alex's transition from the ostensible leader of a gang of outsider girls

Figure 1.3 Alex (left) is confronted by girls in the school bathroom in *Only the Brave*

into a more traditional outsider: rejected by her friends, Alex faces the bathroom of girls (and the implicit world at large) alone (see Figure 1.3).

The scene makes clear the outsider's association with themes of alienation and disaffection and, increasingly, with intersectionality with, in this case, Alex's queerness the site of difference for which she is being punished. Though a now emphatic outsider, however, Alex is neither cowed nor changed. But her falling out with Vicki – Vicki is one of the girls facing off against Alex in this bathroom scene – also leads into the tragic final scenes of the film.

As I noted earlier, fire is associated with Alex's queer desire with shifts from wild blazes to Kate's fireplace symbolising Alex's emerging sexual maturity and control. It is also associated with Alex and Vicki's obverse journeys, and in particular with Vicki's increasing volatility and danger. As Alex's best friend and foil, Vicki's volatile excess is contrasted throughout the film with Alex's comparative control. Vicki drinks to the point of vomiting, she breaks windows, she carries a razorblade and threatens violence, while Alex frequently chastises and calms her destructive behaviours. But most often Vicki starts fires and, over the course of the film, does so as increasingly dramatic responses to emotional flashpoints: when Alex spends the night with Kate instead of her, we see Vicki sitting at a campfire; after Alex accidentally witnesses Vicki's father's abuse of her, Vicki burns down the school library; when Alex eventually finds her after that act, after following a trail of empty petrol cans, Vicki sets herself alight.

Vicki's death occurs on the roof of an empty industrial building at night aside a silent train track. When Alex finds Vicki sitting alone, covered in petrol, on top of the building, she is facing away from her and towards the distant night-time cityscape. Vicki dies almost immediately after Alex's arrival: she clicks a lighter and dies in silence, with Alex's screamed 'no' in the background the counterpoint. Kokkinos uses changes in camera angles and focus to abruptly shift between shots of Alex's reaction, abstract shots of buildings, and extreme close-ups of the flames to explore – albeit less convincingly than in her later films – the visceral experience of trauma for the outsider. The link with Alex's outsider status is emphasised spatially. French (2013: n.p.) argues that Vicki's facing towards the distant cityscape signals these girls' marginalisation and specifically how 'cut off from communities, families, and "the action"' they feel. But while this spatial motif underscores Alex's outsider status – the person closest to her now dead – Vicki's death also newly orientates Alex by giving her a direction, given that she leaves town the following day. As Sara Ahmed (2006: 1) writes, 'To be orientated is also to be turned toward certain objects' and people that 'help us find our way'. Where Vicki could not find her way out of the volatile liminality of adolescence, symbolised by the fire that ultimately consumed her, her self-immolation nevertheless steels and guides Alex to find her way through it and to leave town as the two had previously intended.

Self-immolation is by no means a common feature of coming-of-age films, of course, and is more widely associated with protest and ritual in developing countries (Biggs 2012). In Western popular culture it is typically used as a device in response to 'individual maltreatment or as a means to end intense personal suffering' (Romm et al. 2008: 988), and underscores the connection between sexual abuse and suicide (Bahk et al. 2017). Certainly for Freiberg and Damousi (2003: 221), the scene depicts the Greek body as a 'suffering body' with Vicki's suicide a response to the abuse she suffers at home and the shame she feels at its exposure. Indeed, breaking with stereotypical representations of the Greek family in Australian cinema, 'Vicki's Greek father is portrayed as a sexual abuser rather than an over-protective patriarch' (Freiberg and Damousi 2003: 219). The earlier scene that reveals the sexual abuse shows Vicki calmly waiting for her father to enter her room, bent over and holding onto the end of the bed. When he does enter the room, her bedroom door remains open during the abuse, revealing it as an accepted family ritual rather than a secret act being carried out. This depiction is all the more horrific precisely because of how quotidian it is shown to be. It is when Alex accidentally discovers this abuse by looking through Vicki's window that Vicki, on seeing her friend, becomes dissociative and suicides the following evening. That it is Alex doing the looking, emphasised in an extreme close-up of her eyes, foregrounds the outsider as a witness to traumatic injustice and the failures of institutions ostensibly intended to protect, in this case the family (a motif that, as I discuss in later chapters, re-emerges in Kokkinos's later films). Vicki, then, stands in dramatic counterpoint to Alex's own coming of age, not least because the abuse she suffers and her later suicide represent a tragic perversion of two of the key rites of passage in the genre, namely foundational sexual encounters and the formation of an identity independent of the family (McWilliam 2017b; Goldsmith 2010). In contrast, Alex's sexuality is depicted through standard signifiers of romance (as I noted earlier), while her single-parent family is depicted as safe and comparatively supportive of her independence.

Though quite unlike Vicki's abusive family, Alex's Greek-Australian family is also depicted in ways unconventional for Australian cinema. Alex's Greek heritage is symbolised by absence, and the absence of her Greek-Australian mother in particular. Freiberg and Damousi (2003: 218) write: 'Alex's Greek mother, far from being the loyal subservient wife and mother, has abandoned her husband and daughter.' Though the mother-blame trope is central in *Antamosi*, Alex does not resent her mother for her absence in *Only the Brave*; rather, she longs for her return. Throughout the film, Alex's mother is always shown in a fitted red dress, first in photos and later in memories, which is now Alex's. For Vicki, who tries the dress on in an earlier scene, the dress symbolises the glamorous singer she will never become. For Alex, the dress is a talisman for the return of her mother. Alex recalls a number of memories of her mother in the film, always in the red dress, with two memories in particular cast in blues and greys and occurring at a train station. In the first memory, Alex is on a train and sees her mother on the passing platform; she shouts to her mother, who looks briefly before turning away. In the second, Alex is on the platform and watches her mother sitting beside Alex-as-a-child on a passing train. Neither train stops. The scenes, occurring in the transitional spaces of the train station, cast Alex's relationship with her absent mother as a rite of passage in her coming of age, and specifically her need to let go of her so as to embrace the independent identity symbolic of coming of age. In many ways, then, Alex's mother represents the liminality that threatens to 'shackle' Alex to her past, just as Katina was shackled to hers through her father in *Antamosi*.

When Alex is reunited with her mother in the penultimate scene of the film, as Alex lies in hospital after Vicki's death, the scene recalls Sophia and Katina's reunion in *Antamosi*'s opening scene. In both instances, long-estranged mothers and daughters stare at each other silently without embracing. In fact, there are no words spoken in the scene at all, though Alex's father, mother, and Kate all briefly visit. But unlike Katina, Alex – newly oriented by the trauma of Vicki's death – no longer idealises her parent. The broader silence in the scene thus calls into question institutions of adult authority and especially, as is typical of the genre, school and the family (Gottschall 2010). Vicki's family has abused her to the point of suicide; Alex's mother has arrived too late to parent; and Alex's teacher failed to heed her earlier call for help with Vicki. Alex's 'awakening knowledge' has exceeded that offered by these childhood institutions: she has come of age.

Figure 1.4 Alex's mother's dress hung on the fence at the abandoned shack in *Only the Brave*

The final scene of the film shows Alex hanging her mother's iconic red dress on the fence outside the abandoned shack she shared with Vicki and friends (see Figure 1.4), before leaving town on foot.

By the film's end Alex is no longer in a liminal space: she leaves the symbol of her longing for her mother (and Vicki's longing for a future) on the fence, a boundary marker of her childhood, and walks towards adulthood and independence. The final image of the film is of Alex, first in a close-up and extending to an extreme long shot (see Figure 1.5), as she walks along an empty road, leaving town in perhaps the quintessential rite of passage.

Raffaelle Caputo writes of the genre:

> Imagine the last scene of a film [...] in some lonely country setting. [...] He has a clear view of everything on the horizon, and at times seems as though he can reach out even further. He is at the end of an initiation journey in which, plunged through his first heart-rendering experience, he lost his greatest, most passionate love. The loss precipitates the gain, the experience draws him closer to manhood, and now the world before him opens up to take him in. This is [...] the prototypical image of coming-of-age. (Caputo 1993: 13)

Figure 1.5 Alex leaving town: the final image of *Only the Brave*

Alex, too, has experienced great loss as she walks towards a larger world. And in concluding with such a quintessential coming-of-age scene, it is therefore significant that – for the first time in Australian cinema, at least – it is through a queer, working-class, Greek-Australian girl that Kokkinos has enunciated the genre. And it is a broad configuration that Kokkinos largely returns to in her first feature film, *Head On*, which also employs the coming-of-age genre but with a queer male protagonist.

From *Only the Brave* to *Head On*

Kokkinos's student short *Antamosi* (1991) and short feature *Only the Brave* (1994) both offer insights into her emerging style as she progresses from film student to filmmaker. In this chapter I have been broadly occupied with noting the features and preoccupations of this developing style, in particular her recurrent focus on Greek-Australian migrant characters in working-class Melbourne. However, the Greek-Australian families she depicts across these films vary significantly, in an early hint of the pluralistic and unfixed depictions of Australian identity that Kokkinos's oeuvre collectively reveals. In noting the emphases and preoccupations of these films, this chapter was particularly interested in the emergence and characteristics of the proto-outsider in her oeuvre, emerging first with Katina in the final scene of *Antamosi*, and then with Alex, who begins *Only the Brave* as one of a group of outsiders, before transitioning into a more traditional, lone outsider by the film's end. Both protagonists embody multiple sites of difference as working-class Greek-Australians, while Alex is young and queer, too. And, to different extents, they reveal Kokkinos's emerging constructions of the outsider as specifically intersectional, the sum of complex and 'shifting configurations' of difference (Atewologun et al. 2016: 224). This is perhaps epitomised by Alex's transition into a traditional outsider with the 'outing' of her queerness.

Together, these protagonists also reveal Kokkinos's outsider as an emerging motif for the disaffection and powerlessness of the marginalised, which are epitomised through increasingly dramatic and visceral depictions of trauma: through Katina's untethering to her idolisation of her father, and Alex's witnessing of Vicki's abuse and suicide. The latter in particular reflects the first signs of Kokkinos's outsider as a witness to the failures of hegemonic institutions – here the family and school and, in later films, the police and the government – and a counter-testimony to dominant constructions of Australia available at the time. In many ways, these preoccupations are explored in greater detail, although often in very different ways, in her three feature films. How and to what extent, then, do these features recur in *Head On*? And how does protagonist Ari compare with Kokkinos's female proto-outsiders?

Notes

1   'Most influentially' because *Strictly Ballroom* was not only the most commercially successful of these films – indeed, it is still in the Top 10 'Australian Feature Films of All Time' as ranked by national box office (Screen Australia 2017) – but it also spawned a subsequent film cycle known as the 'glitter cycle' (on which, see Rustin 2001).

2   That the predominant genre used to represent difference in early to mid 1990s mainstream Australian cinema was comedy perhaps underscores the notion that comedy can depict marginal subjectivities in ways that are experienced as less threatening or confronting by the mainstream. A converse explanation is Gilbert's (2004: 166) point, in her discussion of American comedy, that 'comedy creates a "safe" context for the actual hostility and frustration' felt towards 'various groups'.

3   Even so, there have been attempts to reclaim these 'overlooked' 1990s Australian feminist films, as with the University of Sydney's 2016 'FemFlix' exhibition, for more on which, see <https://sydney.edu.au/news-opinion/news/2016/08/02/femflix-revisits-an-overlooked-decade-of-90s-feminism-in-austral.html> (last accessed 12 April 2019).

4   Although I acknowledge Kirkby's (2007) point about the challenges of applying this term to female characters, who have historically been excluded from the grotesque masculinity it has typically revolved around.

5   Though I argue that the queer coming-of-age cycle in Australia only emerged in the 2000s (see McWilliam 2017b), Gottschall (2010: 179–80) has read *Love and Other Catastrophes* (dir. Emma-Kate Croghan, 1996) as a coming-of-age film, which would challenge that argument, though still not precede *Only the Brave*.

6   For an account of post-millennial queer coming-of-age films in Australia, see McWilliam (2017b).

7   Coming out is typically described as the public claiming of a queer identity, though Michael Bronski (2000: 20) notes that it can 'have a variety of meanings and actions: a self-acknowledgment of same-sex desires, claiming the self-identity of being gay or lesbian, acting sexually on these desires or identity, or publicly proclaiming this identity'.

8   This distinction is evident in, for example, *Newcastle* when Fergus's same-sex crush on Andy is taken to mean that therefore 'you don't like girls', as though the two are mutually exclusive possibilities. And in *Monster Pies*, Mike repeatedly 'comes out' after Will suicides, the latter tragically unable to accept his own queer desire. However, as I note elsewhere (McWilliam 2017b), *52 Tuesdays* (dir. Sophie Hyde, 2013) is a notable exception, as is the earlier work of Kokkinos.

Head On: centring the other

Head On, Kokkinos's first feature film and the film for which she is best known, premiered at Cannes Film Festival in May 1998, three months before it premiered in Australia. Within Australia, it was released to frequently rapturous critical responses. For example, Paul Fischer (n.d.) wrote: 'It would be fair to say that with first-time director Ana Kokkinos' audacious work, Australian cinema has come of age.' Paul Byrnes (n.d.b), writing for the National Film and Sound Archive of Australia, was similarly celebratory: 'In terms of iconoclast daring, *Head On* has no equal in Australian cinema.' The film, the third highest-grossing Australian film of the year at the national box office, was nominated for nine awards at the 1998 Australian Film Institute Awards, including Best Achievement in Direction and Best Film. Though *Head On* won only one of those nominations (Jill Bilcock for Best Achievement in Editing), it was nevertheless an emphatic debut onto the national stage for Kokkinos. The film went on to win at least twenty-nine awards nationally and internationally and was distributed relatively widely, securing limited distribution in the United States and, according to Kokkinos (in Krach 1999), fourteen other countries, too. Almost two decades later, the film is now firmly established as a queer classic (Shaw 2012) and continues to be screened around the world, most recently in 2017 at the 8th Kashish Mumbai International Queer Film Festival. *Head On* is perhaps unsurprisingly also the film on which most existing Kokkinos scholarship has focused, although there have still long been questions about the 'surprisingly little academic writing on it', leading Collins and Davis (2004: 159) to speculate that it is 'not only a film about a troubled teen but is itself the troubled teen of 1990s Australian cinema'.

As I noted in the Introduction, much of the existing scholarship on Kokkinos has been interested in the depiction of queerness (Hunn 2000; Jennings and Lominé 2004; Vernay 2006; McIntyre 2010) and/or ethnicity (Tziallas 2010; Papanikolaou 2009; Plunkett 2006; Aquilia 2001; Bennett 2007; Freiberg and Damousi 2002) in Head On. Papanikolaou (2009), for example, considers the film's queering of Greek identity, while McIntyre (2010) examines the spatial mapping of queerness in the film's mise en scène. Across this insightful literature and the varied foci within it, there is frequently an emphasis on the 'interplay between ethnicity, sexuality and nationality' (Tziallas 2010: n.p.). And, in some ways, it is a trend to which I will also contribute. In this chapter, then, I aim to build on existing scholarship by looking broadly at the ongoing development of Kokkinos's style across her oeuvre, while tracking her increasingly bold and visceral focus on the outsider – or 'centring the other'. Indeed, Ari shares key similarities with Kokkinos's proto-outsiders in her early films, as with Ari's social-realist siting in a Greek-Australian milieu in which he does not comfortably fit. But there are key differences from those proto-outsiders, too, among them a greater focus on the visceral, a bolder and less conventional depiction of queerness (including a recasting of the coming-of-age genre through the conventions of New Queer Cinema), and a foregrounded interest in the intersectionality of identity (and of the outsider's in particular).

Head On

Head On is a 104-minute feature film directed by Kokkinos, and adapted for the screen from Tsiolkas's novel by Kokkinos, Mira Robertson, and Andrew Bovell. Like Only the Brave, Head On is a stylised social-realist film that focuses on a queer Greek-Australian youth coming of age in Melbourne. And as with *Only the Brave*, social realism sites this narrative within a working-class milieu and embodied by a socially marginalised protagonist. While the coming-of-age genre often focuses on a number of rites of passage associated with the symbolic transition to adulthood, from falling in love to having sex for the first time (Kitson 2008), Kokkinos focuses on the central rite of passage: namely, the formation and acceptance of an independent identity (Goldsmith 2010; Padva 2004; McFarlane 1987). McFarlane elaborates that in Australian coming-of-age films,

> the issue of personal identity has taken centre stage [and often] emphasize[s] the painful aspects of growing up: the adjustment to Australian mores of children under the influence of other national backgrounds; the rebellion against repressive institutions; the difficulties of coming to terms with parental authority and expectations; the frustrating search for suitable adult models of ways of thinking, feeling, and behaving; and the challenges of adult sexuality. In their various ways, these aspects of growth constitute pressures, tensions, and obstacles that must be taken into account in the move towards self-realization, which is, in so many of the films in this category, the dominant narrative motif. (McFarlane 1987: 134)

Negotiating this rite of passage in *Head On* is Ari (played by Alex Dimitriades), an unemployed queer youth in his late teens who lives at home with his Greek-Australian family comprised of his mother, father, and younger sister. Ari's older brother Peter (played by Alex Papps) lives in a share house with girlfriend Janet (played by Maya Stange) and new housemate Sean (played by Julian Garner). Like *Antamosi* and *Only the Brave*, *Head On* depicts a fraught relationship between Greek-Australian parents and their children, this time between Ari and his father, with Ari's family depicted in 'conventional and stereotypical terms: oppressive father, weak mother, secretly transgressive but overtly compliant children' (Freiberg and Damousi 2003: 219). Indeed, one of the film's foci is Ari's frustration with increasing familial pressure to fulfil hegemonic social and cultural expectations as a young Greek-Australian man:[1] as his Aunt Tasia (played by María Mercedes) puts it, 'Find a girl. Get married. Then it doesn't matter what you do.' But it is precisely this narrative, a narrative that offers Ari what Richard Howson (2006: 143) discusses as 'the process of hegemonic becoming' or 'aspirational hegemony', that Ari rejects and the film problematises.

The film traverses just over twenty-four hours in Ari's life in which his frustration and sense of containment within familial and socio-cultural expectations are contrasted with his mobility and pursuit of pleasures; in some ways, he is an outsider to these expectations precisely because of his privileging of pleasure. These pleasures – his drug-taking, sexual promiscuity (primarily with men), and even his dancing – are physical and reveal the film's visceral emphasis on embodiment. These pleasures are depicted in bolder and less conventional ways than in *Only the Brave*. Where Alex's queer desire was couched within conventional signifiers of romance, for example, Ari privileges the sexual over the romantic and the non-monogamous over the monogamous. This is most evident in his relationship with Sean. While Ari's other sexual encounters are with nameless men and occur around a brief sexual encounter, Sean is presented as a romantic option early in the film. The two talk and flirt, and Sean walks Ari home. The two later begin a sexual encounter at Sean's house. However, Ari becomes sexually and physically abusive at the precise moment Sean romanticises their encounter (Sean declares, 'I think I'm falling in love with you'). The scene concludes with a fist fight and Ari being thrown out into the hallway, naked and alone. For Dyer with Pidduck (2003: 283), here Ari 'chooses the dark pleasures of the sewer over a happy ending'. But it is less a rejection of 'a' happy ending, and more 'the' happy ending, namely the frequent resolution of the classical cinematic narrative in a monogamous romantic coupling.[2]

Head On is thus not simply the coming of age of a queer but a specifically *queered* coming of age, insomuch as Ari rejects fixed identities and the hegemonic narratives and institutions within which they are traditionally couched. Ari's eschewal of fixed identities in *Head On* is, as I noted of *Only the Brave*, quite unlike most queer coming-of-age films of the time which tended to depict a transition from one fixed identity (heterosexual) to another (gay or lesbian) (Padva 2014: 98) and were epitomised by the protagonist's coming out late in the film to claim their new identity (Padva 2004; Bronski 2000). However, Ari neither transitions from one identity to another nor comes out at any point, with his coming of age instead enunciated through the conventions of New Queer Cinema (Jennings and Lominé 2004; Tziallas 2010). 'New Queer Cinema' is a phrase coined by B. Ruby Rich to refer to a body of queer, independent film that emerged at the 1992 Toronto International Film Festival (Rich 1992; Aaron 2004). For Rich (1992: 31), the films shared less a specific style or genre and more an attitude: 'There, suddenly, was a flock of films that were doing something new, renegotiating subjectivities, annexing whole genres, revising histories in their image'. These films explored much more challenging depictions of an increasingly diverse (though still predominantly male-focused) range of queerness than that offered in mainstream cinema, such as in *Poison* (dir. Todd Haynes, 1991), *Edward II* (dir. Derek Jarman, 1991), and *Swoon* (dir. Tom Kalin, 1992).[3]

Though New Queer Cinema is most associated with North American films in the early 1990s, *Head On* has been celebrated as the first Australian exponent of New Queer Cinema. Indeed, the film has been heralded as a 'landmark piece of Australian queer cinema' (McCann 2015: 43), a 'watershed' as the first Australian film to 'compris[e] the key features of New Queer Cinema in its formal inventiveness, its representations of sexualities and sexual desires, and its problematisation of identity politics' (Jennings and Lominé 2004: 147; see also Griffiths 2011). Certainly *Head On* features frequent and visceral depictions of queer sex and sexualities, most frequently casual sex between men, alongside Ari's half-hearted sexual encounter with a female friend. Jennings and Lominé (2004: 147–8) go so far as to argue that '*Head On* is about sex, about Ari's sexual life.' Sex is often a standard feature of the coming-of-age genre: it is a rite of passage in which the male protagonist's first sexual experiences often symbolically correlate (however dubiously) to 'becoming a man' (McWilliam 2017b). In *Head On*, however, sex is not a rite of passage. Rather, Ari's promiscuity and privileging of sex over romance de-signifies sex from its role in hetero- (and homo-)normative romantic and coming-of-age narratives.

In a genre in which sex is not just a rite of passage but, for Gottschall (2010: 178), the 'central' rite of passage, *Head On* offers a significant queering of what it means to 'come of age' in Australian cinema through its emphatic privileging of fluidity over fixity. Certainly Ari eschews fixed identities and the hegemonic narratives and institutions within which they are traditionally couched, in which romance leads to sex leads to marriage leads to procreation – what Ahmed (2006: 173, 201) describes as the 'set points' on the 'straight line' of the heteronormative life narrative. Ari's deviance from this narrative is flagged from the very first scene, which quickly establishes the queer gaze and offers viewers a queer orientation to the film. In the first scene Ari leaves a Greek wedding (a scene I note later) to pursue queer sex in a public toilet. The public toilet scene is shot in a series of slow-motion extreme close-ups, slowing down time to focus desirously on, for example, an anonymous man removing his belt. In combination with an exaggerated use of sound – the heightened sound of a zip being opened, for instance – the scene viscerally enacts a sense of sexual anticipation which both establishes Ari's queer desire for the man, but also renders the audience complicit in that desire as we watch Ari's anticipation and pleasure. The latter is made explicit as Ari masturbates (in a full-frontal shot) the next morning, which also flags Kokkinos's much bolder and more explicit approach to the depiction of sex and sexualities in *Head On* than in her previous films. As Jennings and Lominé (2004: 149) note, '*Head On* as a whole then appears a cinematographic attempt (for the first time in Australia) to define or rather illustrate what queer means in practice, not as a concept but as an embodied experience.'

While her depiction of an embodied queer experience has been considerably less prominent in existing discussions of her work, Kokkinos's broader visceral approach has been much remarked upon. Critics and scholars alike have frequently described *Head On* in terms of its physical impact: it is 'exhilarating' (Pomeranz and Stratton 2016: n.p.), it 'enters the realm of the senses' (Buckmaster 2014: n.p.), it is a 'high-velocity assault' that, through '[t]echniques such as hand-held camera, tight, claustrophobic framing and rapid editing emphasise the visceral nature' of 'sex, drug-taking, music, dancing and violence' (Collins and Davis 2004: 158). To these techniques I would also add the use of intense colour and sound, and slow motion: techniques that collectively draw attention to and immerse the audience in the physicality of Ari's story. Kokkinos's visceral filmmaking does not construct just an embodied queer experience, though, but also a queer spectatorial orientation by contrasting an embodied queerness to a disembodied, problematised heterosexuality. For example, Ari's cousin (and hetero-foil) Joe (played by Damien Fotiou) becomes engaged early in the film – engagement being precisely the 'set point' on which Ari is currently being pressured. However, there is no flirting, desire, or intimacy – no embodied sexuality on display, as might be expected of a young couple celebrating their engagement – between Joe and new fiancée Dina (played by Dora Kaskanis). Rather, there is emotional and physical distance and, at times, overt resentment and frustration between the two. It is later revealed that Joe only became engaged because Dina's parents promised to buy them a house. By actively problematising a disembodied heteronormativity while centring the film around an embodied queer point-of-view, *Head On*, as Luke Mancuso (2010: 97) writes of *Brokeback Mountain*, positions viewers 'on a slanted line, an oblique sight line that disfigures the straight lines of dominant viewer identification'.

For Ahmed (2006: 177–8), such an orientation is queer and thus disorientating: 'queer lives are about the potentiality of not following certain conventional scripts of family, inheritance, and child rearing, whereby "not following" involves disorientation'. It is not insignificant, then, that Ari also spends much of

Figure 2.1 Ari disorientated on a drug high in *Head On*

the film disoriented: outside of his broader disorientation from heteronormativity, his disorientation is frequently underscored by disorientating uses of sound (Ross 2012), while he is also frequently disorientated under the influence of drugs. Late in the film, for example, Ari is coming down from a high: he is shown in a deep red hue as he hugs himself and stares blankly at the night-time cityscape he passes as he is roughly pulled forward by unseen forces (see Figure 2.1).

The scene conveys the disoriented state of Ari's drug high, as well as specifically associating it with queer culture: drag queens blow him kisses as he passes. Though Ari's disorientations are often self-destructive, the film's frequently visceral association between queerness and disorientation nevertheless invites the audience to take Ari's perspective: to take up the queer spectatorial position introduced in the first scene so as to experience the film (and the world?) aslant. The outsider in *Head On* is thus both queer and queerly disorienting.

Ari is first introduced as a queer outsider in the very first scene of the film. After the opening credits, which I discuss later, the film begins with Ari dancing at the reception of a Greek wedding – one of the standard tropes of 'Greekness' in Australian cinema (Freiberg and Damousi 2003). While Ari initially dances in the middle of the frame and in the middle of a circle, he soon stops dancing and leaves the circle. Ari looks on from the periphery of the room towards the circle where Ari's father is pinning money to the bride and groom: a celebration of the heterosexual Greek-Australian couple. Tziallas (2010: n.p.) notes: 'He is now literally and figuratively on the margins with the heterosexual couple symbolizing the pinnacle of where his spiraling movements were supposed to lead him eventually: heterosexual marriage.' When the bride's garter is later thrown to the unmarried men in the room, Ari turns his back and leaves the building to instead pursue queer sex in a public toilet. He is outside the rituals, spaces, and expectations of his family and friends, having turned his back on the 'set points' of Ahmed's 'straight line'. And, as I note later in this chapter, Ari chooses to remain outside those set points when his coming of age culminates in his acceptance of an emphatically queer identity in the film's final scene.

As with Kokkinos's proto-outsiders in her earlier films (see Chapter 1), the outsider in *Head On* is also a witness to trauma, and this time a specifically queer trauma. Late in the film Ari and transgendered friend Toula/Johnny (played by Paul Capsis) goad the police while high. The police take immediate exception to Toula and the two are taken into custody, revealing how 'the state still punishes sexual transgression' (Tziallas 2010: n.p.; see also McIntyre 2009). Taken into a white room, Ari and Toula are told to remove their clothes by two male police officers, a senior Anglo officer and a young Greek-Australian officer. When Toula refuses to remove her underwear – removing her underwear would reveal her genitals and challenge her performance of 'Toula', forcing a 'conflict between [. . .] her feminine identification and a still masculine body' (Hunn 2000: 124) – she pleads in Greek with the young officer. However, Toula's address to him in Greek establishes a link between them that the senior officer uses to question his colleague's hetero-masculinity: 'You better help her along,' he says, 'Seems she knows you.' Admonished with the taint of queerness, the young officer roughly strips Toula before repeatedly beating and kicking her amid a stream of insults ('You're a whore, you're a disgrace'). Ari briefly attempts to come to her aid, but is warned off and tearfully watches on, naked and cupping his penis in a sign of his sudden impotence, a stark contrast to his emphatic queer virility in preceding scenes. While Ari is a victim, he is also, and perhaps most emphatically, a witness: watching on as his friend is violently assaulted by transphobic police, in ways not dissimilar to Alex witnessing Vicki's abuse at the hands of her father in *Only the Brave*.

In *Head On*, then, the figure of the outsider is again used to explore the alienation, disaffection, and powerlessness of the socially marginalised, which culminates in a trauma caused by a figure of authority (fathers in *Antamosi* and *Only the Brave*, police officers in *Head On*). In this way, the outsider functions as a witness to, and critique of, the confronting failures of hegemonic institutions in the Australian cultural landscape. But here, more so than in Kokkinos's previous films, there is a foregrounded exploration of the intersectionality of identity within these themes. It is specifically Toula and the young officer's shared Greek heritage, for example, which triggers the brutal transphobic attack. Joanne Nagel writes:

> Sexual depictions and denigrations of racial, ethnic, and national 'others' and the regulation of in-group sexual behavior are important mechanisms by which ethnic boundaries are constructed, maintained, and defended. Race, ethnicity, and the nation are sexualized, and sexuality is racialized, ethnicized, and nationalized. (Nagel 2001: 123)

But it is Ari's negotiation of the intersectionality of his own identity which receives the most attention in the film, including: his age and gender as a young man; his socio-economic status as an unemployed person from a working-class family; his cultural heritage and experience in a troubled, multi-cultural Australia; and his sexuality as a queer who pursues non-monogamous sex. For Dyer with Pidduck (2003: 280, 283), Kokkinos's key contribution to New Queer Cinema is precisely that her films 'facilitate a much more complex understanding of the articulation of race and ethnicity to national identity, gender and sexuality' in such a way that 'unsettles normative social structures, tidy endings and stable identity formations alike'. Indeed, in many ways *Head On* epitomises Kokkinos's exploration of the outsider as the sum of complex, socio-culturally situated, and 'shifting configurations of inequality along various dimensions' (Atewologun et al. 2016: 224).

This foregrounded exploration of the intersections of identity is reflected in the film's structure, which in some way literally layers different 'sections' of identity against each other. The first and last scenes of the film, for example, are key queer moments: Ari begins the film by leaving a hetero wedding to walk into the night to secretly pursue queer sex, while Ari ends the film dancing in the morning light in an acceptance of his non-monogamous queer identity. But the film is also more broadly book-ended through its opening and closing credits that comprise black-and-white montages of immigrants at Melbourne Port, framing Ari's queer coming of age within a context of dislocation, change, and identity negotiation. Evangelos Tziallas writes:

> Images of mothers, fathers and their children standing in front of a large ship poignantly communicate a feeling of displacement. From the opening montage, Kokkinos foregrounds the importance of family, and its relation to identity as a result of the immigrants' displacement. The use of black and white photos signifies history and memory, and when combined with the non-diegetic music and dissolves, creates a sense of nostalgia. (Tziallas 2010: n.p.)

But it is less 'a sense of nostalgia', which might imply a wistful or contained view of the past, and more a framing of Ari's queer coming of age within a broader context of cultural dislocation, troubled multiculturalism, and explicit identity negotiation. This is taken up in different scenes throughout the film, but perhaps most explicitly in a scene in which Ari joins Peter's friends, who are chatting about race, racism, and immigration:

> Ariadne: That's what's wrong with this country. Everyone hates everyone. The skips hate the wogs, the wogs hate the Asians . . .
> Ari: And everyone hates the blacks.
> Ariadne: Yeah, exactly.
> Ari: You don't even know any Kooris.
> Ariadne: What's that got to do with it? I fight racism wherever I see it whether it's the Greeks, the Italians . . .
> Ari: Fuck the wogs.
> Ariadne: . . . the Vietnamese . . .
> Ari: Fuck the gooks.
> Ariadne: . . . or the Kooris.
> Ari: And fuck the boongs.
> Ariadne: What's your problem? What are you, Ari, some kind of wanker?
> Ari: [chuckles]
> Ariadne: So fuck everyone else. You're proud to be Greek.
> Ari: Proud to be Greek? I had nothin' to do with it.

It is, of course, not insignificant that Kokkinos sites such an explicit problematisation of multiculturalism and identity at a Greek club in urban Australia. Here the story of migrants is, quite unusually, being told by migrants and their descendants, rather than by the white, Anglo-Irish everyman that Australian cinema has historically privileged. And, indeed, Sean – the only Anglo participant in the broader discussion – is also depicted as the most out of touch with multicultural reality: he begins the discussion by noting that 'there shouldn't be any barriers [to immigration]. The idea of a nation-state's a thing of the past.' But Ariadne and Ari's exchange reveals Sean's liberal discourse to be naive and reflective of considerable social privilege.

For Bennett (2007), the exchange highlights a number of issues that collectively point to a much more complicated understanding of multiculturalism – and, by extension, intersectional identity – being offered than that offered in other popular Australian films of the time. Films like *Strictly Ballroom*, as noted in the previous chapter for example, offer what Bennett (2007) terms a 'good multiculturalism' in that they offer positivist depictions based on a paternal 'tolerance' of difference, and are often told from the perspective of ethnically unmarked protagonists. In *Head On*, however, Kokkinos offers no such positivist depictions and instead positions ethnic subjects as the challenging and imperfect authors of their own histories. The exchange between Ariadne and Ari, for example, problematises the notion of multiculturalism by drawing attention to the frictions and fissures between and within ethnic groups, and concludes with Ari's refusal to celebrate an ethnocentric identity. In doing so, Ari reveals his 'own conflict of identity' around the boundaries and intersections of multicultural, second-generation, queer 'Australian-ness' (Bennett 2007: 71–2). For Bennett in his compelling discussion (2007: 71–2), this works to open up a more productive, even optimistic space for thinking about multiculturalism (and, I might argue, identity in general) in Australia:

> Ari's rejection of political debate and his identity as either explicitly Australian or Greek consequently creates space for another way of conceiving identity. [...] Later [Ari] returns to the table and says to Ariabi [sic]: 'Fuck politics, let's dance!' Thus a Bakhtinian approach is enabled, allowing the film to present national identity from the margins as something that is not 'concrete' and well established but is discursive, multiple, even oppositional: something stood outside of. (Bennett 2007: 71–2)

Importantly, Kokkinos does not resolve this problematisation of identity at the end of the film, but rather foregrounds its 'multiple, even oppositional' strands. Indeed, the last scene of the film is interesting for a number of reasons. The scene occurs at a wharf at dawn and is intercut with black-and-white images of migrant arrivals at a wharf (book-ending the film's contextualisation within cultural displacement, but perhaps also the hope of transition). As Ari walks to the wharf, we see the cityscape behind him (see Figure 2.2).

Figure 2.2 The cityscape behind Ari on the wharf in *Head On*

French (2013: n.p.) has argued that 'looking from the largely industrialised west at the city' is a spatial motif that Kokkinos uses to underline how her 'characters feel cut off from communities, families, and "the action"' and, in *Head On* in particular, 'signif[ies] the divide between the west and the centre'. While French's argument is a convincing one, and indeed there are earlier scenes where Ari looks towards the city from the west,[4] I think there is an additional reading in this scene in particular. While Ari has felt displaced from, and an outsider to, 'communities' and 'families' throughout the film, it is not insignificant that in this last scene of the film he is walking *away* from the city. He has, both literally and metaphorically, turned his back on 'the centre' and its hegemonic conventions and scripts. As Ari's father may have arrived at that wharf for a new beginning, so too does Ari arrive at something like a new acceptance of himself as queer. For instance, where Ari's opening monologue revealed his frustration with social and familial pressure to meet Ahmed's 'set points' on the heteronormative 'straight line' – job, marriage, children – Ari's final monologue concludes with: 'I'm gonna live my life. I'm not going to make a difference. I'm not going to change a thing. No one's going to remember me when I'm dead. I'm a sailor and a whore, and I will be until the end of the world.' In his queered coming of age, rather than transition through this liminal stage Ari instead chooses to stay in it: to live his life aslant.

The use of 'sailor' and 'whore', two figures associated with the wharf and that connote mobility and promiscuity, is reinforced while Ari drops to his knees during his voice-over to, it is implied, give oral sex to an anonymous man at the wharf (McIntyre 2009). The scene then cuts to Ari dancing a *zeibekiko* alone on the wharf as a crane-shot pulls away and up, our last image of him a slow-motion dance with his arm and face raised to the sky at the dawn of a new day. Where Ari snuck away into the dark in the first scene of the film to pursue queer sex, here he faces a new day perhaps not triumphantly, but certainly resolute in his acceptance of an independent, queer identity: Ari has, in short, come of age (Padva 2004: 355; McFarlane 1987). Berry tentatively agrees:

> on the visual level, it invokes all the liberatory imagery of rite of passage films, with Ari standing alone on a dock, turning circles as the camera cranes above him. However, instead of a 'positive image' affirming his freedom and faith in the future now that he has 'found himself' and 'begun to come out', Ari's voice-over statement is a far more ambiguous assertion of self-determination. (Berry 1999: 37)

There is no 'coming out' because, as I argue at the beginning of this chapter, *Head On* is not simply the coming of age of a queer but a specifically *queered* coming of age. As Collins and Davis (2004: 162) note of the film's last scene, as 'a coming-of-age moment this is a wonderfully perverse image' precisely because it 'refuses to submit to the genre's tendency to look back, to reassure its audience, to satisfy the patriarchal, heterosexist fantasy of familial unity'. The scene also, to return to Bennett (2007), refuses to resolve the broader problematisations of identity that the film so frequently poses. In his earlier exchange with Ariadne, for example, Ari rejected the idea of being proud of his Greek heritage and yet he ends the film engaged in a traditional Greek folk dance. Certainly the scene (and film) offers a queering of Greek-Australian identity, diversifying what it means to 'come of age' in Australian cinema (Papanikolaou 2009). But more than that, in choosing not to resolve the identity issues she raises – there is no neat resolution where the aspects of Ari's identity suddenly align unproblematically – Kokkinos insists on identity as multiple, overlapping, and discursively constructed, which is embodied by the first (and most) emphatically intersectional outsider of her oeuvre.

Head On towards *Revelations*

In many ways, Kokkinos's celebrated first feature film *Head On* (1998) builds directly upon the characteristics and preoccupations tentatively developed in her earlier films, namely her student short *Antamosi* (1991) and short feature *Only the Brave* (1994). Certainly *Head On* expands upon Kokkinos's earlier uses of stylised social realism and her focus on Greek-Australian migrant families in working-class Melbourne, which are explored through protagonists who are variously outsiders to their families, communities, and society more broadly. *Head On* also expands on the emergence of the queer outsider coming of age in these milieus, which she originally explored in *Only the Brave*. But in *Head On* Kokkinos takes a much bolder and more visceral approach in focusing on the promiscuous, drug-taking experiences of her protagonist Ari: *Head On* offers less the coming of age of a queer, then, and more a specifically *queered* coming of age. In doing so, Kokkinos offers the first Australian contributions to New Queer Cinema, positioning the outsider as both queer and queerly disorientating and offering viewers a queer spectatorial position from which to view the film (and the world?) aslant.

But it is sometimes a traumatic viewing: like Kokkinos's proto-outsiders in *Antamosi* and *Only the Brave*, Ari is also a witness to trauma, and this time a specifically queer trauma when he and friend Toula/Johnny are arrested and forced to strip naked by police, and Toula is viciously beaten by those police in a transphobic attack. The effect is that the figure of the outsider again functions as a witness to the confronting failures of hegemonic institutions in the Australian cultural landscape: parents in *Antamosi* and *Only the Brave*, police officers in *Head On*. But unlike those earlier films, *Head On* also uses the outsider as a pretext to consider the failures of inclusion within those institutions by foregrounding the intersectionality of identity. One of the central foci of the film is precisely the frictions between the different elements of Ari's identity as a young, queer, Greek-Australian man expected to marry a woman and have children. This emphasis on intersectionality is also reflected in the film's very structure, which book-ends Ari's queer coming of age within the context of the film's opening and closing credits of migrant arrivals at Melbourne Port. But where Kokkinos has 'centred the other' in her first three films in ways that increasingly emphasise the intersectionality of the outsider – epitomised here in *Head On* – what then of Daniel in *The Book of Revelation*, who is a privileged, middle-class, heterosexual, Anglo-Australian man?

Notes

1 Because Ari is in his late teens, he is both a 'teen' and a 'young adult'. This does not impact my reading of the film as a 'coming-of-age' film. As Driscoll (2011: 22) notes, the 'lack of clear distinction between teenagers and young adults [. . .] is in fact a recurring feature of teen film'.

2 Hardwick (2009: 39) also notes that Sean represents the film's 'potential love story'.

3 These films arose out of a much longer 'tradition of lesbian and gay film-making within the history of independent, experimental and "outsider" cinema' (Rich 1992: 30), a filmmaking tradition that has been documented in texts like Vito Russo's *The Celluloid Closet* (1981), Richard Dyer's *Now You See It* (1990), Andrea Weiss's *Vampires and Violets: Lesbians in Film* (1993), and Dyer's edited collection *Gays and Film* (1977). See Aaron's (2004) *New Queer Cinema* for an extended discussion.

4 Tsolkias's book is divided spatially between different parts of Melbourne, each of which has a distinct character, though my interest here is exclusively in the film.

The Book of Revelation: othering the centre

With Sharon Bickle[1]

The Book of Revelation, Kokkinos's second feature and her most controversial film to date, premiered in Australia at the Melbourne Film Festival in July 2006. Released eight years after *Head On* (1998), *The Book of Revelation* spent most of those intervening years in development (Byrnes n.d.a; Cordaiy 2006). One challenge was adaptation: Kokkinos and Andrew Bovell adapted the film from Rupert Thomson's 2000 novel of the same name, including transposing the story from Amsterdam to Melbourne, the site of all of her fictional films. Another challenge was financing. Even for Kokkinos, who had emerged with such resounding success on the national stage with *Head On*, *The Book of Revelation* was a tough sell to financiers. As Byrnes (n.d.a) offers, Kokkinos's 'films are more formally adventurous and self-conscious than most of her contemporaries, and more difficult to finance'. Certainly as an art-house rape-revenge film *The Book of Revelation* was some distance from the commercial, genre-based filmmaking that the Australian film industry was shifting towards at the time (a shift epitomised by the 2008 founding of Screen Australia).[2] It is perhaps unsurprising, then, that where *Head On* was released to frequently rapturous reviews, particularly in Australia, Kokkinos's follow-up was received tentatively and, even now, remains widely regarded as an anomaly in her otherwise highly regarded oeuvre.

This dynamic is also reflected in scholarly engagement with the film. More than a decade after its release it is still the focus of only a handful of discussions published in trade magazines and scholarly books and journals. Of this existing work, most has focused on the film's engagement with the rape-revenge genre[3] (Heller-Nicholas 2011a, 2011b; Henry 2013, 2014; McWilliam and Bickle 2017), and particularly its reversal of gendered norms: its replacement of a female rape victim with a male, and male perpetrators with females. In this chapter, we aim to expand this genre work into an examination of both the characteristics and preoccupations of the film, as well as its place within Kokkinos's broader oeuvre. In doing so, we are interested in examining how the film does indeed depart from many of the trends established in Kokkinos's earlier films, most notably her previous emphases on social realism, Greek-Australian milieus, and queer coming of age, yet still conforms in key ways with her emphases on sex, trauma, and outsiders. We are particularly interested in the depiction of the film's protagonist Daniel (played by Tom Long) who, as a successful, white, hetero-masculine man is the only hegemonic protagonist of Kokkinos's oeuvre. In particular, we argue that Daniel's abduction and torture disorientates him so profoundly that he is rendered an outsider to his own life – he changes his name and leaves his previous job, house, partner, and profession on his return from captivity. Further, we argue that the film's close focus on the vulnerable heterosexual male body, and particularly its privileging of spatial relations, presents rape as a trauma of disorientation – a sort of vertigo – in which the victim is unable to reassert control and achieve stability, even after his release. Daniel's experience of rape fundamentally alters his sense of place and hence his understanding of himself in the world, to the extent that he is traumatised into becoming an outsider. Directed by and towards his unknown attackers, the three masked women, Daniel's relationship to his body and masculinity is transformed; his ability to make meaning of people and objects is lost. Only through Mark's (Colin Friels) intervention does the film end with the promise of Daniel's restored masculinity. Thus, where Kokkinos's previous films increasingly focused on an intersectional outsider (or centring the other), *The Book of Revelation* can be read as the reverse: as 'othering' the standard hero of much Australian cinema, namely the 'white, heterosexual man of Anglo-Irish origin as the Australian type par excellence' (Seco 2008: 145). We examine how this occurs in relation to its revisioning of genre, its use of space, and its emphasis on disorientation.

The Book of Revelation

Unlike Kokkinos's three previous films, *The Book of Revelation* is neither set in a working-class Greek-Australian milieu nor organised around an intersectional protagonist, both of which had emerged as her directorial signatures by 2006. Instead, the film begins in the privileged world of modern dance and centres around a celebrated Anglo protagonist. But Daniel's privilege is soon challenged when he undergoes a series of violent abuses. Indeed, *The Book of Revelation* is a 113-minute rape-revenge film that employs a stylised or art-house realism, alongside stylised dialogue and minimal or discordant music. Set in Melbourne, the film follows Daniel who, with girlfriend Bridget (played by Anna Torv), is the principal dancer in a modern dance troupe directed by Isabel (played by Greta Scacchi). After a rehearsal in the first scene of the film, Daniel walks to the shops and is abruptly abducted in an alleyway by three masked, cloaked women. Daniel spends twelve days in captivity, which are revealed slowly in increasingly intense flashbacks, and it is this captivity and its impact on his (and others') life that is the film's focus.

As its biblical title suggests, Daniel experiences a personal apocalypse during his captivity: he is chained to a floor, raped, and tortured. On his release, Daniel is unable to explain what has happened to him; he leaves Bridget, stops dancing, and embarks on a violent quest to find his attackers, who remain unidentified throughout his abduction and throughout the film. Instead, he searches for women with similar features: a butterfly tattoo, red fingernails, red hair. When Daniel begins a relationship with Julie (played by Deborah Mailman), he begins to reclaim parts of his life, including a tentative return to dance, in part because the casting of an Indigenous actor allows him to trust that she was not one of his attackers. However, Daniel is far from recovered and, when he violently attacks a woman in a nightclub after mistaking her for one of his attackers, he is arrested. It is only then, his abductors still unknown and at large, that Daniel seems as though he may finally be able to communicate his traumatic experience to Mark, a sex crimes detective and Isabel's ex-partner.

The film marks Kokkinos's first use of the rape-revenge genre, a genre that emerged in 1960 with the release of Ingmar Bergman's *The Virgin Spring* – a director Kokkinos has noted as an early inspiration (Kalina 2009) – though it was not until the 1970s that the genre achieved widespread popularity, at least in the United States (Clover 1992: 138; Lindop 2015: 55; Heller-Nicholas 2011b). Although still associated with the 1970s (Projansky 2001: 60), the rape-revenge genre has recently undergone another surge in popularity with films like *The Last House on the Left* (2009), *I Spit on Your Grave* (2010), *Straw Dogs* (2011) – all three of which are remakes of 1970s rape-revenge films of the same name – alongside *Descent* (2007), *Teeth* (2007), and *The Book of Revelation*. Like most rape-revenge films, *The Book of Revelation* is organised around 'a rape (or many rapes, or an attempted rape) and an act of revenge' (Heller-Nicholas 2011b: 3). These events are narratively organised across three acts: 'rape, transformation, revenge' (Read 2000: 242). In the first act, the protagonist is raped (or almost raped); in the second act the protagonist undergoes a recovery, whereby they slowly transform from victim to avenger; and in the third act, they seek and enact revenge, often raping and/or murdering their attacker in the penultimate scene (Read 2000: 242; Heller-Nicholas 2011a: 88).

In *The Book of Revelation*, these acts are intercut with Daniel's captivity and are told in flashbacks throughout the second and third acts of the film. The effect is, rather than emerging from captivity into a clear revenge phase, Daniel remains lost: confusion and disorientation stay with him. Even at the film's end, the motives and identities of his attackers remain unclear, not only to Daniel himself but the audience: this is reinforced when we learn in the credits that Anna Torv plays both girlfriend, Bridget, and the attacker, Gertrude. Though Kokkinos has insisted there is no narrative link between the two characters (Hopgood 2006), nevertheless the reimagined spaces of rape not only remain, and continue to affect Daniel, as well as extend beyond the diegetic world of the film.

Unlike most rape-revenge films, however, *The Book of Revelation* reverses the typical emphasis on male perpetrators and female victims (Heller-Nicholas 2011a, 2011b; McWilliam and Bickle 2017). Byrnes (n.d.a) argues that the film is 'based on a simple, powerful idea: most films about rape are about women as victims of men, so reversing that idea allows men to experience the trauma of violation'. And it is through that trauma that, as we argue throughout this chapter, it is the hetero-male body that is rendered vulnerable and Daniel who is violently remade into an outsider. But unlike the characters of Kokkinos's other films, who are marked by diverse intersectionalities but who frequently demonstrate considerable resilience, Daniel remains vulnerable: broken and unable to adapt to his new situation.

The film itself opens on a rehearsal focused on Daniel and Bridget who, like the heterosexual newlyweds at the beginning of *Head On*, are also at the centre of the frame and again suggest the primacy of heteronormativity. Certainly Daniel is a stereotypical lead; young, white, and muscular, he is both popular with and desired by other dancers. The opening scene offers a split screen: the camera follows Daniel as he moves through the dance studio, revealing the bodies of the other dancers flexing and stretching. The use of Daniel's point-of-view establishes Kokkinos's visceral approach, as well as introducing bodies – working bodies as objects shaped by and for work – and their orientations as a key feature in the film. This attention to physicality and purpose contrasts with the dialogue, which is minimalist and often phrased in questions: 'Can you buy me some cigarettes?'; 'Where have you been?'; 'Why are you doing this?' Language in this film marks relationships in terms of uncertainty, particularly Daniel's relationships with the female characters (Bridget, Isabel, his attackers). In contrast, the rehearsal establishes the centrality not of Daniel's perspective (the scene is shot behind Daniel's head) but his body. A physical hierarchy is established: Daniel directs a harnessed Bridget confidently and pushes down male dancers. When Isabel reprimands Daniel after an overtly sexual thrust, her demand that he dance 'without ego' draws attention to his (hetero)sexuality and the way it overshadows and dominates the bodies of the other dancers. After the rehearsal, Bridget asks Daniel to buy her cigarettes and it is on his way to the tobacconist that an abrupt fade to black marks the moment he is abducted.

The following scenes are of Isabel's and Bridget's concerns when Daniel does not return for the evening's performance. But we do not immediately see where he is; in fact, the next time we see Daniel he is being pushed out of a moving van in an isolated dirt field beside a train track, his head covered in a hessian bag in the first, and quite literal, indication that Daniel has been disoriented by his capture. It is also the first hint that Daniel has been rendered an outsider, from having started in the city centre in a position of control and privilege to being pushed into the dirt on the outskirts of the city. French (2013: n.p.) writes: 'After his kidnap and rape, Daniel is dumped in the west of Melbourne like rubbish – perhaps signifying the west of the city as a wasteland.' Where *Head On* concluded with Ari walking away from the city, choosing to embrace a disorientated worldview (in Ahmed's sense of it) and to live aslant (see Chapter 2), Daniel walks towards the city with a newly disorientated worldview that has instead been thrust upon him by trauma and abuse.

On his return home, Daniel is unable to tell Bridget what has happened, which at this point is also unknown to the audience. Claire Henry (2014: 128) notes that the audience 'feels Daniel's trauma, coming to know he has been raped before seeing the visible proof of the rape scene'. Indeed, Daniel is now both effectively mute and unable to sleep; he flinches at light and at sudden movement. Daniel's fragility is symbolised by glass: his return is marked by Bridget breaking a glass decanter and Isabel later breaking a wine glass. Not only is the fragile uncertainty of connection through language lost, he also loses the ability to dance – an action over which he previously held mastery. When he returns to rehearsal, he stands impassively looking helplessly down at his body (via a disorienting camera shot down his body at the clothed bulge of his penis) before leaving.

Daniel's twelve days of captivity, seen in flashback, involve a series of assaults, from being physically stimulated against his pleas to being forced to masturbate and later raped and tortured, chained to a wall from his penis. During his forced masturbation early in his captivity, Daniel reasserts his subjectivity by telling the women 'when a man fucks a woman, no matter how beautiful she is, whenever he closes his eyes he always thinks of himself'. This briefly reinstates the male as active (the one who 'fucks') and beauty as a passive quality possessed by women. This stands in contrast to the women's answer to his early question 'Why me?', which is 'Because you're beautiful.' His claim to control an internal space, and assertion of the primacy of his relationship to his penis, is brutally countered when he is raped with a large strap-on dildo. After he is sodomised, his attacker says, 'You know what you are, don't you? You're a cunt.' This shift of Daniel's status from active to passive, from male to female, reasserts the conventional gender relationship familiar to the genre, and marks the point of transformation in Daniel's subjectivity. His hegemonic privileges are being forcibly removed from him: he is being 'othered'. As Kokkinos (qtd in Cordaiy 2006: 41) notes, the abuse scenes are 'about power and the reversal of power [. . .] his power position as a man is stripped away from him'.

Further, it is power that Daniel does not recover on his release, where he is instead increasingly an outsider to his own life. Indeed, once released, far from emerging from captivity to embrace the conventional role of avenger, Daniel's search is chaotic: he is no longer fit for purpose as a dancer, but neither is he an effective tool of revenge. Daniel leaves Bridget, and has sex with multiple women in a search for his attackers. This search, however, lacks narrative coherence as the distinguishing marks of his attackers – red hair, red fingernails, a circle tattoo on a breast, a butterfly tattoo on a hip – do not resolve the identities of the attackers, but instead remain random fragments that resist organisation and closure.

While seduction is frequently an element in the revenge act (Lehman 2001: 7; Henry 2013: 141), the intimacy of Daniel's search for his attackers creates an increasing 'tension' around the 'threat of vengeful violence' (Henry 2014: 132, 133). In seeking to avenge his rape himself, Daniel's revenge quest is consistent with films like *Kill Bill Vols. 1 & 2* which feature the rape victim avenging the attack themselves. As Projansky (2001: 60) notes, there are two main variants of the genre, depending on who avenges the rape. In one variation, the avenger is typically a man who has lost his 'wife or daughter to a rape/murder', as in *The Virgin Spring, Braveheart,* and *Memento,* and in the other, the avenger is the victim themselves, as in *Lipstick, I Spit on Your Grave, Ms. 45,* and *Kill Bill;* in both variants, however, the victim is a woman and her attacker a man or men (Projansky 2001: 60). Indeed, 'the most immediately recognizable instances of the rape-revenge film are [. . .] structured around a male perpetrator and a female victim' (Heller-Nicholas 2011b: 9). That Daniel is both victim and avenger is thus of note. In fact, the gender reversal and attendant shifts it triggers offers a reimagining of the genre itself, for as Andrew Urban (2006: n.p.) notes in his review of the film: 'We see many films about men using and abusing their power over women, rarely the reverse. And never like this.'

Henry (2014: 127, 130) agrees that *The Book of Revelation* offers a reimagining of the genre (it is what she terms a 'revisionist rape-revenge' film), though she argues that this is primarily because of its 'sensitivity' to depicting the experience of a male rape victim, as well as its emphasis on the subsequent post-traumatic impact on his life. However, we argue that its 'reimagining' extends beyond these aspects. It is not only highly unusual for its gender inversion of victim and attackers – in the small number of rape-revenge films where the victim is male, the attacker is also male (for example, *Deliverance, Acolytes, Vulgar,* and *I'll Sleep When I'm Dead*) – but also because its victim is a masculine, heterosexual man. Male victims in rape-revenge films are typically marginalised or 'othered' in some way, usually constructed as either a 'feminised' man or a child (Lehman 2001: 75; Heller-Nicholas 2011b: 50). In *Deliverance*, for instance, the victim is overweight, feminised Bobby, whose marginalised status is flagged by his attackers when they note 'Looks like we got us a sow here instead of a boar' (Schubart 2007: 86; Cohen 2014), while in *Acolytes* the victims are teenagers. In *The Book of Revelation*, however, Daniel's muscular body and heterosexual desirability are emphasised from the very first scene of the film, first during the dance rehearsal and later when a fellow dancer flirts with him. Even so, any expectation that Daniel's masculinity and heteronormativity might translate directly into a more satisfying revenge narrative is frustrated. While Daniel quickly turns to violence as a means to reassert himself, his masculinity, and his mastery of his world, his inability to accurately identify his attackers means this violence remains unfocused and unresolved, and extends the impact of the original rape by creating new victims from his (falsely) retributive assaults. Thus, rather than depicting revenge as an effective counter-narrative to rape trauma, the film instead suggests that revenge is a site of further trauma, an expansion of the initial crime. In terms of the rape-revenge genre, then, *The Book of Revelation* denies the role of revenge as a form of return or reinstatement of the status quo: instead, the outcome of rape is a rolling state of trauma.

The film's title also flags a broader reimagining. The biblical Book of Revelation, the final book of the New Testament, presents the prophetic visions of John, events that describe an apocalyptic vision of death and destruction and the second coming of Christ. At the centre of the film is Daniel: not only is the film's narrative fixed on Daniel in terms of his psychological development but, particularly in the captivity scenes, Daniel's naked male body, trussed or hanging, is literally the centre of the room and the centre of frame. At the centre of his body, his penis, and the power struggle over who controls it, means that while he is the victim, Daniel's body/the naked heterosexual male body is never de-centred or marginalised, even while Daniel himself struggles to understand his place post-rape. In this sense, the male body is the film's 'text', the visionary 'Book of Revelation' and that which is revelatory. The portentous title both indicates the power rape has to wreak destruction, and points towards what is revealed: a post-rape world that, regardless of the intervention of the Christ-like Mark, remains scarred by the horrors that have been witnessed.

What is also significant for this reimagined post-rape world is the contrast between the rape narrative as it is written on the naked male body and the way in which the raped female body exists in other films. Thus, while the raped male body describes and defines a profound disorientation in the world, in other films, even the recent *Mad Max: Fury Road* (2015) – a film lauded for its presentation of female subjectivity – raped, tortured, and traumatised female bodies are used as a generic strategy to orientate the audience, invoking a familiar post-apocalyptic world, with motherhood and milk symbolically affirming the subjugation of humanity to the alien-looking Immortan Joe and his War Boys. Therefore, by associating rape with the male body rather than the female body, Kokkinos finds a space to redefine rape as a site of unresolvable trauma, but also, problematically, raises questions about the raped female body as decentred and normalised: little more than apocalyptic mise en scène. As Kokkinos herself offers, 'Man as victim, women as perpetrators seemed such a bold idea. The simple reversal invites us to look at the situation through new eyes' (qtd in Urban 2006: n.p.). One of the things those 'new eyes' reveal is the cultural intersections between rape and gender that become apparent when gender norms are reversed.

In focusing attention on the heteronormative male body as the location and interpretative framework for the experience of rape, Kokkinos not only redefines the rape-revenge genre, but presents a new vision of the post-rape experience as a traumatic reimagining of the world. A phenomenological reading of the film using Ahmed's notions of queer phenomenology reveals how rape trauma can be usefully interpreted in the film as a problem of orientation. From his original position as the dominant male (the site of 'ego'), Daniel does not emerge in the revenge act, as we might expect of the genre, loosed from the ties of relationship and moral responsibility, newly shaped to the purpose of vengeance. Indeed, the complicated structure of the film in which Daniel's rape/s are shown in flashback means that clear boundaries between the rape and the return are impossible to establish. The film thus raises questions about when, and if, Daniel re-emerges at all. In this way, Kokkinos resists the genre's simple stages: the narrative movement which displaces the trauma of rape with the subsequent atonement of revenge. Instead, Daniel has been knocked askew, trapped in a world defined by dislocation. Daniel's experience of rape redefines his world but not in simple, purposeful ways. Instead, he is effectively ejected from the life he previously lived: he is rendered an outsider to his own life.

Ahmed (2006: 25) describes phenomenology as a 'turn toward' objects. Traditional phenomenology concerns itself with the experience and perception of objects (Cerbone 2006: 3), and Ahmed refines this, using not only the work of Husserl and Heidegger but particularly Merleau-Ponty's work on embodiment, to focus on orientation as a way of knowing where we are: both spatially and in terms of sexual orientation. Ahmed (2006: 5. 68) argues that bodies 'become orientated by how they take up time and space' and 'orientations toward sexual objects affect other things that we do such that different orientations, different ways of directing one's desires, means inhabiting different worlds'. In this way, Ahmed defines the queer of 'queer phenomenology' as a departure from the straight, not only in sexual terms, the differences between normative and non-normative sexual identity, but also more broadly as a way of being in the world, of facing the world aslant. The spectre of a world reshaped by violent disorientation is raised, but itself exists aslant to the main interest of her work. It is these largely unexplored implications of disorientation as a violent reimagining of the world, and of the subject's altered place within it, that we are interested in in this chapter.

In the film's opening scene, there is a direct relationship between body and purpose – dance is less performance and more a way of being and mediating the self as subject, although the scene of fans by the studio door reinforces the success of Bridget and Daniel's embodiment of gender roles through dance. Daniel's view of the world as revealed by dance is not so much black and white as up and down: he orientates himself to those around him hierarchically by pushing the harnessed Bridget firmly upward, and the male dancers down. Daniel's dance has a clear, vertical axis and direction. That this also reflects the orientation of his life is made clear when, after the rehearsal, Daniel walks across Melbourne to the tobacconist. The vertical architecture of the city reinforces the upward trajectories of the dance: the eye is drawn up by the sky above the narrow laneway he walks through, and follows the upward flight of pigeons (see Figure 3.1). This is punctuated by the downward slam of a window signalling his abduction.

If, in Ahmed's terms, it is our orientation to material objects – tables, chairs, doors, windows – that determines the way we act and think in the world, then the shift from the vertical orientation of the early scenes to Daniel lying horizontal on the floor in his

Figure 3.1 An emphasis on the vertical early in *The Book of Revelation*

Figure 3.2 Daniel's shift to 'horizontal' after his capture in *The Book of Revelation*

captivity (see Figure 3.2), his wrists and ankles bound, becomes highly significant. A ballerina in a music box sits just out of his reach, a symbol that Daniel is now his captors' plaything, which is emphasised when he asks why they have abducted him and is told, 'For our own pleasure.' The shift of orientation from vertical to horizontal can thus be interpreted as Daniel's transformation from subject to object. Ahmed argues:

> The upright body is involved in the world and acts on the world, or even 'can act' in so far as it is already involved. The weakening of this involvement is what causes the body to collapse, and to become an object alongside other objects. (Ahmed 2006: 159)

The masked women's final assault is to chain him to the wall by a cock ring until he dances for them, which he does, as they remind him he is 'powerless'. Whereas previously Daniel's muscular dancer's body affirmed his primacy and his dominance, Daniel's dance confirms his transformation: locked alone in the centre of a small room, bound wrists attached to a chain in the ceiling, Daniel hangs, unnaturally and awkwardly upright, rather than stands. At the end of his dance, he spins ineffectually, confirming his collapse into object as he embodies the containment and purposelessness of a music-box figure.

In returning to 'ordinary' life, Daniel is unable to return his world to an upright perspective. Bridget contributes to the blurring of the boundaries between captivity and release through a shift in the film's colour palette. The oranges of the early scenes are now reds (in chairs, furnishings, and in Bridget's dress) which invoke the distinctive red nails of one of his captors. Moreover, Bridget is far from sympathetic to the returned Daniel. When Bridget returns home to find Daniel naked asleep in bed (on sheets and pillowcase with vertical stripes), she pulls the sheet from him and thrusts him onto the floor in an echo of his captive (horizontal) position. The blurred boundaries between captivity and ordinary life emphasise Daniel's rape as a trauma of disorientation – a shift to a world that does not or cannot right itself. Daniel's initial return to his life is characterised by failure: he is unable to account for his missing time; he is unable to dance (the means by which he previously asserted his masculinity and a reflection of his emasculation by his female abductors); and, despite his rising tally of anonymous sexual partners, he is unable to find his attackers. Even in the final moments of the film, when Daniel thinks he has found one of his attackers, he is wrong. Daniel follows a red-headed woman into a toilet, violently hitting and undressing her as he searches for a tattoo. When he fails to find it, he abandons the attack but is literally expelled from society – he is chased down by members of the public before being locked in a police cell – his quest to find his attackers unachieved. The moment, occurring in the final two scenes of the film, marks Daniel's transition to outsider as complete. That Daniel's revenge is ultimately unsuccessful also underscores the complexity of enacting his revenge in a traumatised post-rape world.

There are two attempts to re-anchor Daniel after he has begun to seek out his attackers. Through Mark, a dying Isabel re-establishes contact and invites Daniel and Julie to lunch. Her act of reconciliation is presented as a maternal act: Daniel recognises the familial associations when he jokes to Julie, 'it's not like you're meeting my mother or anything. Isabel's much worse than my mother.' While Daniel's reconciliation with

Isabel aids his recovery – he tentatively returns to dance – this is upset when he is arrested. This sets up the final attempt to re-anchor Daniel when Mark – the film's paternal figure as well as, in terms of the broader biblical association of the title, a Christ-figure – visits Daniel after his arrest in the final scene. Mark hugs a stricken Daniel, holding him upright, literally offering Daniel the support to reorientate himself from object (horizontal) to reimagined subject (vertical). Mark then invites Daniel, in the last words of the film, to 'go back to the beginning': to tell his own story. This suggests that, with Mark's help, Daniel might be able to finally assert a coherent narrative framework for all of those fragments, and thus re-establish control. In this way the film ends with the possibility of Daniel reorienting his disoriented masculinity.

From revelatory to *Blessed*

As a rape-revenge film, *The Book of Revelation* represents a confronting departure from many of the genre's heteronormative foundations. In its replacement of a female (or even marginalised male) rape victim with a dominant, heterosexual male who is then unable to successfully enact his revenge, Kokkinos explores a new space for the genre, one that resists a simple progression from rape to revenge such that revenge somehow atones for the trauma of rape. Instead, *The Book of Revelation* depicts rape in terms of violence and dislocation which, read through Ahmed's notions of orientation, reimagines Daniel's world, profoundly altering his relationship to his body and to the people and practices that had previously anchored him in his life. The effect is that Daniel – violently stripped of his privilege in his abduction and progressively rejecting, or ejected from, every one of the connections of his previous life – is remade into an outsider who is, at the film's end, literally locked away from society. In some ways, then, the only hegemonic protagonist of Kokkinos's oeuvre becomes the most explicit outsider in it.

Certainly *The Book of Revelation* shares with Kokkinos's previous films a focus on a traumatised outsider. Moreover, the outsider again functions as a witness to the failures of hegemonic institutions in the Australian cultural landscape: the family in *Antamosi* and *Only the Brave*, and the police in *Head On* and *The Book of Revelation*, the latter when Daniel decides against reporting his abduction to the police when two male police officers laugh at his suggestion that a male could be abducted by women. The moment underscores the failings of fixed or hegemonic notions of gender and identity, offering another facet to Kokkinos's interest in diversifying conceptions of Australian identity, and rendering vulnerable and powerless the most privileged subject in Australian cinema. Indeed, it is possible to read the film as a violent rejection of masculinist Australian film mythologies. At the very least, where Kokkinos's previous films increasingly focused on an intersectional outsider (or centring the 'other'), *The Book of Revelation* offers the reverse: an 'othering' of the standard Australian cinematic hero, the white, hetero-masculine man (Seco 2008: 145).

But while *The Book of Revelation* shares a number of foci with Kokkinos's previous films, it is nevertheless an anomaly, too: Daniel is a privileged subject whose story is neither set in a Greek-Australian, working-class milieu nor told using the conventions of social realism. But these are conventions that Kokkinos returns to, to different extents, in her final film, *Blessed*. However, unlike *Antamosi*, *Only the Brave*, and *The Book of Revelation*, each of which focuses on a single outsider protagonist, *Blessed* focuses on an ensemble of outsiders comprised of a group of teenagers and their mothers.

Notes

1   This chapter has been redeveloped from our earlier article originally published as:

McWilliam, Kelly and Sharon Bickle (2017), 'Re-imagining the rape-revenge genre: Ana Kokkinos' *The Book of Revelation*', *Continuum: Journal of Media and Cultural Studies* 31.5: 706–13, <http://dx.doi.org/10.1080/10304312.2017.1315928>.
Reprinted by permission of the publisher (Taylor & Francis Ltd, http://www.tandfonline.com).

2 For an account of this shift, see McWilliam and Ryan's *Australian Genre Film* (Routledge, forthcoming).

3 We acknowledge the work of scholars like Clover (1992, 1993) and Creed (1993), who have discussed rape-revenge as a sub-genre of horror, and Read (2000), who has discussed it as a narrative pattern across genres. However, in this chapter, we follow Claire Henry (2014: 4), who sees rape-revenge as a specific genre that has emerged from horror but has developed its own narrative, stock characters, themes, and iconography.

4

Blessed: an ensemble of outsiders

Blessed, Kokkinos's fifth film and third feature, premiered in Australia at the Melbourne International Film Festival in July 2009 and was released nationally two months later. Though released only three years after *The Book of Revelation*, *Blessed* was in development for eight years (Mitchell 2017). As with *The Book of Revelation*, most of those years were spent securing funding and adapting the film from its literary source. Indeed, the film is based on the 1999 Australian play 'Who's Afraid of the Working Class?', written by Melbourne Workers' Theatre writers Andrew Bovell, Patricia Cornelius, Melissa Reeves, and Christos Tsiolkas with composer Irine Vela. The screenplay, initially developed by Bovell, Cornelius, Reeves, and Tsiolkas, was eventually finalised by Bovell who took over as lead writer (Cordaiy 2009). Where the play combines four distinct stories – 'Suit' by Tsiolkas, 'Money' by Cornelius, 'Dreamtown' by Reeves, and 'Trash' by Bovell, which collectively offer a 'portrait of working-class life in Australia' (Production Notes[1]) – the screenplay was reorganised around the central theme of mothers and their children on Kokkinos's direction (with the film's title drawn from one mother's description of her children as her 'blessings') (Cordaiy 2009).

Unlike *The Book of Revelation*, however, *Blessed*'s lengthy development was overwhelmingly well received. With a rating of 85 per cent on rottentomatoes.com, *Blessed* was widely considered a 'return to form' for Kokkinos after the polarising and 'alienating' *The Book of Revelation* (Hopgood 2009: 17). Indeed, the film was popular on both the national and international film festival circuits (Gonzalez 2009), winning, for example, the Jury Prize at both the San Sebastián and Kosmorama Trondheim Film

Festivals. McFarlane (2010: 88) goes so far as to describe *Blessed* as 'a *great* film, and it is not often one would risk that degree of praise'. Kokkinos, too, considers it a 'knock-out film', the 'best I've ever done' (qtd in Buckmaster 2009: n.p.). Nationally, the film's profile was likely helped by its casting of a number of high-profile Australian actors, including Frances O'Connor, Deborah Lee-Furness, Miranda Otto, and William McInness. The film was nominated for four awards at the 2009 Australian Film Institute Awards, including Best Film (although curiously not also 'Best Director'), Best Lead Actress (Frances O'Connor), Best Adapted Screenplay, and Best Editing. The film ultimately won one of those awards (Best Lead Actress), but notably did so against larger and higher-profile films, including Baz Luhrmann's *Australia* and Bruce Beresford's *Mao's Last Dancer*. Even so, *Blessed* has been, at least for Dominic Barlow (2015: n.p.), 'all-but-forgotten' by the film-going public in the intervening years.

Blessed is similarly yet to secure any substantial interest from scholars with only a handful of journal articles or book chapters focusing on the film (e.g. French 2012, 2013; Ross 2012) outside of the more numerous, though equally insightful, reviews, essays, and interviews with the director (e.g. Cordaiy 2009; Hopgood 2009; McFarlane 2009). I am informed by all of these writers as I attempt here to examine the characteristics and preoccupations of the film, as well as its significance within Kokkinos's broader body of work. In doing so, I argue that the film offers a key shift from the patterns established in her previous films, but particularly *Antamosi*, *Only the Brave*, and *Head On*. Specifically, where these films focus on intersectional outsider protagonists, *Blessed* disperses these diversities across an ensemble of outsider characters. In this chapter, then, I am interested in both the features and implications of this expanded focus.

Blessed

Blessed is a 110-minute stylised social-realist melodrama. While Kokkinos employs social realism in most of her preceding films (see Chapters 1 and 2), *Blessed* marks her first use of melodrama, a genre that has been employed by filmmakers – albeit in diverse and diversely discussed ways – since the beginning of cinema (Mayer 2018). Contemporary melodrama is best known for the employ of 'excessive emotions' and 'equally excessive music' in the domestic sphere of the family (Williams 2011: n.p.). While social realism and melodrama have historically been associated with different stylistic and thematic preoccupations (Neale 2004; Gledhill 1991), including in Australian cinema specifically (O'Regan 1987), scholars have increasingly pointed to the ways that these filmmaking traditions have been used in combination to tell particular kinds of stories. Laura Mulvey, for example, writes:

> realism and melodrama are, in different ways, stylistically important for dramas of social oppression and injustice. Realism records the state of things, without stylistic intrusion into a representation of the norms of everyday life and its fragile survival strategies. These are conditions that lack buffer zones or safety valves; misfortune or error can quickly mutate into disaster leaving its victims struggling to comprehend, unable to articulate clearly their suffering or the strain that leaves close relationships fissured. It is here that melodrama serves its purpose and the cinema takes on an expressive function that responds to both the intensity of the crisis and its protagonists' desperation. (Mulvey 2013: 1)

There are a number of influential examples of social-realist melodramas, among them the work of Ken Loach (Leigh 2002; Martin-Jones 2009). Loach, for example, employs this hybrid in his 'melodramas of protest' (Leigh 2002). Where social realism typically sites a marginalised protagonist within a realist aesthetic and working-class milieu (Hallam and Marshment 2000), melodramas of protest use heightened emotion to 'invite viewers to experience, through their engagement with characters, [the] impossibly difficult situations and events' of these characters (Martin-Jones 2009: 180). The purpose of this is to 'rouse not just the people in the film, but those in the audience as well'

(Walker 1982: 14) to the plight of these characters and, in particular, the broader socio-cultural injustices to which they are subjected (Leigh 2002).

In *Blessed*, these 'plights' are embodied by intersectional outsiders, a focus Kokkinos returns to after forcibly marginalising the privileged in *The Book of Revelation* – although she does so here in less emphatic ways than in *Head On*. Certainly intersectionality is not consistently foregrounded as a narrative tension for every protagonist as it was for Ari in *Head On*, which is perhaps inevitable given the number of characters. Indeed, where *Antamosi*, *Only the Brave*, and *Head On* focus on an intersectional outsider, *Blessed* disperses this interest in identity across twelve characters: five mothers and their seven children. Rhonda (Frances O'Connor) is a pregnant mother of three on welfare, who has been in a series of abusive relationships with men. The eldest of her children (who does not appear in the film) is in foster care while her youngest children – teenager Orton (Reef Ireland) and younger sister Stacey (Eva Lazzaro) – live together on the streets so as to avoid Rhonda's current boyfriend. When Stacey gets her first period and does not know what to do, Orton calls his mother to angrily remind her that Stacey needs her and it is that call that triggers Rhonda's late-night search for them. Bianca (Miranda Otto) is an unemployed single mother who drinks and plays the 'pokies' (slot or fruit machines), despite the unpaid bills and adult responsibilities she ignores. She is a 'tragic figure, incapable of assuming the responsibilities of motherhood' and 'clearly mourning her own lost youth' (Hopgood 2009: 16). Bianca's daughter Katrina (Sophie Lowe) is a self-sufficient high-school student, although with friend Trisha (Anastasia Baboussouras) is quickly in trouble with the police after skipping school and shoplifting. Trisha's mother Gina (Victoria Haralabidou) is a hard-working Greek-Australian widow, who sews school uniforms for the private school to which she cannot afford to send her own children. Gina is mourning the loss of her husband and the absence of teenage son Arthur/'Roo' (Eamon Farren) who has run away from home. It is not revealed in the film why Roo ran away, though the Production Notes reveal it was to escape his mother's 'cloying love'.[2] Roo, a queer teenager, is shown doing a video interview for what he thinks is a modelling assignment but is actually for an amateur pornographer. Tanya (Deborra-Lee Furness) is also a hard-working mother, working lengthy hours as a carer but still desperately struggling to pay the mortgage alongside unappreciative and unemployed husband Peter (William McInnes). Their teenaged son Daniel (Harrison Gilbertson) leaves the house angrily after being accused of stealing Tanya's next mortgage payment – it is later revealed to have been taken by Peter, who gives it away at a pub – and attempts to reactively rob elderly neighbour Laurel (Monica Maughan). Laurel, too, is a mother although to an adult son from whom she is estranged: James (Wayne Blair) is an Indigenous man whom Laurel adopted as a child. Both Laurel and James are haunted by Laurel's refusal decades earlier to allow James's Indigenous birth mother into his life.

This focus on parallel mother–child relationships in *Blessed* extends upon Kokkinos's broader interest in familial frustrations and particularly the mother–child relationships in *Antamosi* and *Only the Brave* (see Chapter 1). Collectively they reveal 'concerns central to her oeuvre, including an interest in female perspectives, trauma, identity, working-class life, and parental influence on relationships' (French 2013: n.p.). With James and Laurel the middle-class exceptions, other characters are shown either to have no money or to be in an intense struggle for it, which influences their actions over the course of the narrative. Hancock (2014: 35) writes that the 'characters in *Blessed* are represented as both victim of or reactive to their socio-economic situations'. These 'socio-economic situations' are initially reflected in setting. Characters mostly occupy grim, state-provided apartments and a series of run-down houses, alongside the liminal spaces of the 'streets of the city and suburbs' through which the children 'roam' (French 2013: n.p.). The latter emphasises not just the mobility of youth, a feature of *Only the Brave* and *Head On* too, but also that these children are all variously 'lost' and have to 'find their way home' (as per the film's promotion). Unlike Kokkinos's earlier protagonists who rejected or moved away from family spaces, *Blessed* is thus centred in familial relationships and their return/resolution with all of the children beginning the film fleeing (or having fled) the family home, and all but two returning by the film's end.

These relationships are depicted over the course of a day and night and are told twice: the first part of the film is told from the perspective of the seven children (labelled on an intertitle as 'The Children'), and the second half from the perspective of the mothers (labelled on an intertitle as 'The Mothers'). One effect of this is that, where *Antamosi, Only the Brave*, and to a lesser extent *Head On* were all told from the perspective of a child, *Blessed* is structured around a symbolic dialogue between children and their mothers. This structure also reveals the unreliability of narration insomuch as, as I note later, the children's accounts offer an initially limited perspective that depicts the mothers in consistently damning ways, while the mothers' accounts offer a fuller picture of the realities of motherhood and marginalisation. These stories are visually united through a motif presented in montages at the beginning and end of the day in both parts. At the beginning of each part, the featured characters are shown asleep (or ostensibly asleep) in morning sunlight, and at the end of the day, the featured characters are shown in the setting sunlight. Kokkinos has noted:

> It was a structural device to unify all the characters' experiences but we wanted to do more than that – it's almost a meditation on their faces. [...] it's a moment of epiphany, realisation. For the kids, they are all, at that moment, in that day, in some form of jeopardy, in peril, and we are allowed into what the kids are sensing. There is something internal going on which is quite profound. Then when you experience it with the mothers, there's a level of wisdom or sadness for the women in terms of what is actually going on. (Kokkinos qtd in Cordaiy 2009: 20)

These sunlit close-ups of faces also presage the film's extended focus on intimacy and intimate relationships, which are embodied by the mother–child relationships of the film (Rhonda–Orton,

Rhonda–Stacey, Tanya–Daniel, Gina–Roo, Gina–Trisha, Bianca–
Katrina, and Laurel–James, but perhaps also by the absent
relationship of James and his unnamed biological mother).
Also present in these montages are shots of the city, whether
as a background and context for these characters' stories or
as the focus of the shot. These moments reflect not just that
these characters are among the many, often invisible working-
class stories in the city, but also the ever-present dangers such
marginalised characters face. One way this is signalled is through
setting: the areas of the city the characters occupy are ominous
and dilapidated, such as dark alleyways of graffitied brick walls and
damaged garage doors that stand amid deep shadows – areas of
the city that forebode risk. Another way this is signalled is through
the use of sound. As Ross (2012: 61) writes, 'On the city streets,
police sirens enunciate danger, urgency and emergency' which
'reflect the trauma of characters' lives'. Kokkinos thus reinforces
the 'relationship between, and impact of, social environment
and marginalisation on character and identity', rendering these
'socio-economic impacts emotionally intelligible, through the
foregrounding of affective moments' (Hancock 2014: 133).

For each of the families in the film, these 'affective moments'
culminate in varying crises for the children that are triggered by
an event with their mothers, demonstrating that it is 'the mother
characters' who are actually 'the nexus' of the film (Hancock
2014: 132), and often of the melodrama more broadly (Parkinson
2010: 120). For example, in *Blessed* Daniel overdoses on drugs
and is rushed to hospital after becoming angry at his mother,
Tanya, and acting out with fatal consequences: Laurel dies from
an accident when the reactive Daniel pushes her and she falls and
hits her head. When James is asked to identify adopted-mother
Laurel's dead body, he rejects her ('she's not my mother') and
instead goes in an emotional search for connection with his
biological mother. Katrina and Trisha are arrested by police for
shoplifting and taunted as 'trash', after acting out against their
seemingly disinterested (Bianca) or overcritical (Gina) mothers.
After leaving home to escape Gina's apparently overbearing love,
Roo wanders drunkenly through the night after being deceived

into a videotaped performance by an amateur pornographer. Finally, Stacey reveals to Orton the sexual abuse she suffered at the hands of Rhonda's boyfriends, for which Orton angrily blames his mother; refusing to go home, the two fall asleep beside a candle and ultimately burn to death in a goodwill clothing bin (poignantly labelled 'homeless').

These crises foreground and problematise constructions of motherhood within the heightened emotions of the melodrama, with each of the children's perspectives casting the women as ostensibly 'bad' mothers. The 'good' mother, for Arendell (1999: 3), is a white, married, heterosexual woman who is both financially dependent upon her husband and solely occupied with the task of mothering, although Goodwin and Huppatz (2010: 2–3) argue that there are in fact 'variations on' this theme, such as with the 'good working mother'. Key is that the good mother is 'self-sacrificing, devoted and passive' and her emphasis is on nurturing her family – the 'family unit' being the 'foundation of society' (Pascoe 1998: 6). Moreover, this focus must also fulfil her emotionally. A good mother is thus a happy one, whereas 'an unhappy mother is a failed mother' (Johnston and Swanson 2003: 23). In contrast, the mothers of *Blessed* are consistently marked by sites of difference (Greek-Australian and/or working-class and/or single); are responsible for financially providing for their family (even where there is a husband as with Tanya's unemployed husband); and are frequently unhappy, exhausted, and otherwise resigned to their variously challenging lives. Moreover, as working-class mothers trying to financially provide for their children, they are also unable to sustain a sole focus on their children – what Margaret Pomeranz (2011: 248) has described as 'loving neglect' – with perhaps the welfare-dependent Rhonda and elderly Laurel the exceptions.

These characteristics of the 'bad' mother are epitomised by Rhonda, who is the most vulnerable and most explicit outsider of all of the mothers. She is also the dramatic centre of the film: her story both concludes the film and frames it, with the film's title taken from her two descriptions of her children as her 'blessings'. Rhonda begins the film depicted in the least empathetic manner of all of the mothers. We first meet Rhonda, who is heavily pregnant, waiting to see new social worker Gail (played by Tasma Walton), in a dingy government building. When the two meet, Rhonda is abrasive and hostile at the prospect of losing government payments with eldest child Mickey (who does not appear in the film) now in foster care. Though it is not revealed why Mickey was removed from Rhonda's care, it is an early sign that she is a 'bad' mother, reinforced when her younger children are shown sleeping under a pier. Mitchell (2017: n.p.) argues that Rhonda is 'reconciled to the fact that the streets are a safer environment for her children than her own home and compromised brand of care'. While Rhonda drops her defensive posturing briefly in their meeting to note that 'those kids are my blessings – every one of them a blessing', she bristles at the idea that her daughter could be 'assessed' for learning difficulties because 'my whole life is one big assessment'. Rhonda leaves soon after, lighting a cigarette as soon as she is outside, in another suggestion that she lacks genuine care (or skills in caring) for her unborn child. Of all the mothers, Rhonda is the stereotypical 'bad' mother – the 'epitome of the white trash stereotype' (Mitchell 2017: n.p.) – whom the audience is invited to judge in a provocative invocation of the mother-blame trope.

The first act of the film thus broadly recalls E. Ann Kaplan's comments on mothers as:

> always in the margins, always not the topic per se under consideration. The mother, that is, was generally spoken, not speaking [...] She was a figure in the design, out-of-focus; or, if in focus, then the brunt of an attack, a criticism, a complaint, usually in the discourse of a child (male or female) or in that of an adult (male or female) concerned to attribute all ills to the mother. An absent presence, then. (Kaplan [1992] 2013: 3)

In *Blessed*, all of the mothers are initially offered in the first act of the film as 'the topic' under consideration and the cause of their children's 'ills'. For Kokkinos, however, offering the first act from the children's perspective is a strategy through which to problematise the mother-blaming trope and broader patriarchal discourses on mothers and motherhood (Reimer and Sahagian 2015). In interviewing Kokkinos, Mitchell (2017: n.p.) writes that the 'first of the film's acts deliberately withholds information, cannily testing prejudices and judgement', to which Kokkinos adds:

> That was deliberate. You make a whole lot of judgements about the mothers in the first part of the film, but then as you progress through the story, those judgements get turned on their head. These mothers are just as vulnerable as the children that they care for. (Kokkinos in Mitchell 2017: n.p.)

The second part of the film thus allows the mothers to 'speak' for themselves, which complicates the mother–child relationships initially set up by revealing the 'impossible demands of motherhood' (Hopgood 2009: 16) through the 'mother characters' subjective situations' (Hancock 2014: 133). The effect of this is that in revealing the mothers as as much marginalised outsiders as their children, Kokkinos undermines the mother-blaming trope set up in the first half of the film. For example, Tanya may have wrongly accused Daniel of stealing money, but she is an exhausted bread-winner working long hours to keep the family home, while her unkind, unemployed husband threatens to take the house away from her while stealing her money, blaming his son, and gifting it to strangers. These women are, by and large, doing the best they can with the skills and knowledge they have in the moment. But they are also very clearly 'on the social margins' and 'in the cracks of normative society' (Hancock 2014: 133). Even Laurel, who lives in what was obviously once a grand home, now shuffles barefoot through the run-down hallways in a nightgown: she is alone, rejected by her adopted son, and haunted by past deeds as she slips in and out of dementia. In many ways, the film's focus is precisely on the impact of this marginalisation, of being an outsider, on mothers, children, and the relationships they share. And as with Kokkinos's previous films, this culminates in a traumatic experience.

In *Blessed*, this is again epitomised by Rhonda and marks a shift in balance away from social-realist conventions and further towards melodrama: 'There is, of course, an implicit chronology in this dual [social-realist melodramatic] style: in the order of the narrative, the melodrama takes over from realism's depiction of a day-to-day state of things' to express the 'intensity of the crisis and its protagonists' desperation' (Mulvey 2013: 1). In the first half of the film, Rhonda's pubescent daughter Stacey reveals to brother Orton that she has been sexually abused by Rhonda's boyfriends, including her current boyfriend Nathan. Orton assumes that this, too, is his mother's fault. But in the second half of the film we see that Rhonda is likely a victim herself (she is fearful of Nathan when he becomes impatient) and had no knowledge of Stacey's abuse. Indeed, when Orton confronts her about it, she is horrified. Rhonda immediately goes searching for Orton and Stacey along dark streets, asking after them at shopfronts, and 'roaming' the streets like most of the children of the film who are 'lost' and have to find their 'way home'. In doing so, Rhonda walks past the large clothing bin in which her children reside without realising, indicating that these are 'character types who are generally invisible', even to each other (French 2013: n.p.).

Unsuccessful in finding her children, Rhonda returns home and throws her boyfriend's belongings out on the footpath. It is sometime during this expulsion that her social worker arrives with police to tell her that her children have died in an accidental fire in that clothing bin: in the moment Rhonda reorientates herself towards her children, and away from her abusive partner, she has lost them. Hopgood (2009: 17) notes that 'mothers are forever being punished by the loss of their children' in melodramas, including specifically in melodramas of protest in which the 'death of the "innocent", or indeed, innocents' (Walker 1982: 14) is a standard convention. In *Blessed*, it is the youngest children or the ostensibly most innocent that die. At the morgue we see a large, misshapen object under a sheet – the fire has 'fused the bodies together', the attendant explains – before it cuts to a close-up of Rhonda's face. During a brief conversation Rhonda is adamant that the bodies are not to be separated, concluding with: 'they're my blessings, and you're not to touch them'. This is the second time she describes her children as 'blessings', with her descriptions effectively book-ending the film; it also signals a belated retaking of parental and personal agency. Rhonda lets out a series of grief-stricken wails, and Kokkinos offers a prolonged focus through extreme close-ups of Rhonda cross-cut with the reactions of those in an outside room who are horrified to hear her grief. The effect is a visceral emphasis on Rhonda's trauma, which 'calls upon us' to recognise her love for her children and 'to share her grief' (Hopgood 2009: 17): to empathise and look with, rather than at, the outsider.

In rousing us to empathise with Rhonda as the least empathetic and most explicit outsider of all of the mothers, Kokkinos employs a final melodramatic convention to the death of the innocents: namely, the redemptive death. The 'redemptive death' occurs when the 'death of the most virtuous character' has a ripple 'effect on surviving characters (often transforming or saving them somehow)' (Soltysik 2008: 167). In *Blessed*, it is Rhonda's children's death that redeems her in the final two scenes of the film: first at the morgue, and finally at a club on her way home. For one thing, when Rhonda wails in grief, it is arguably the first time she has been 'heard' in the film; Ross (2012: 53) argues that the film features 'characters struggling to be heard, and whose regular pathways of communication with others have been disrupted, obscured or ignored', often as a result of their various marginalisations. For Rhonda, we have seen her feel defensive and 'assessed' rather than productively enabled by the government institutions designed to support her, while she and her children fail to 'hear' each other for most of the film. But here she is seen and heard by numerous characters, retaking her agency (or 'voice'). For another, it is Rhonda's grief that unites brief cross-cuts that reveal the varying reconciliations across the remaining mother–child relationships of the film: Daniel recovers from his overdose and is reunited with Tanya and Peter; Trisha and Gina reconcile and Roo returns home; Katrina is brought home and reunited with Bianca;

and James recovers a cherished artefact from his birth mother. But it is the final scene that best signals Rhonda's redemption.

In the final scene, while being driven home, Rhonda insists on stopping at a dingy pool hall/club. While she has acted in self-destructive ways in previous scenes, that is not the case here. The lyrics of the song playing ('Elsie' by Australian rock band The Divinyls) narrate a tragic working-class life with lyrics such as 'She never had an education', 'Clinging to the edges', 'The world's a hard place to land on', 'In her squally little slum'. The song explicitly frames Rhonda as a poor and vulnerable outsider, as does her context in a gritty, run-down pool hall, collectively reflecting the 'politics' of the film of 'giving voice to those on the very margins of contemporary society' (Hancock 2014: 131). It is the first part of the chorus playing – 'Life can be lonely / Life can be very sad' – when grieving Rhonda walks towards the dance floor. Rhonda first dances energetically throwing her head and arms around in a seeming attempt at catharsis, 'obliterating the pain with bodies in movement' (Krauth 2009: 27), before slowly swaying and holding her heavily pregnant stomach. The light on her face in the club is not unlike the sunlight of the film's visual motif, revealing this moment as the conclusion to the larger narrative of mothers and children (Cordaiy 2009). As the music begins to fade out, the image shifts to an extreme close-up of Rhonda's face, mascara smudged and a tear rolling down it. The scene concludes with a brief silent image of Rhonda's grief-stricken face (see Figure 4.1), Gail offscreen watching on, as we hear a single breath before it cuts to the closing credits.

Rhonda has been locked in a passive cycle of being 'assessed', dispossessed from the narrative of her own life. But in these final moments Rhonda retakes her agency and we are asked to empathise with her. Ross writes:

> By the time the score finishes, we are engulfed by silence, hearing only the sound of Rhonda's breath. With no sound left but the restrained quietness of Rhonda's breath, this suggests that we are right there with her in this moment. (Ross 2012: 64)

Figure 4.1 Rhonda in the final image of *Blessed*

The scene thus continues Kokkinos's approach in *Antamosi*, *Only the Brave*, and *Head On* of asking the audience not to look at outsider protagonists, but rather with them: to view her films from the margins. French argues that:

> Kokkinos has two aspirations: firstly, to realistically represent what for her is a disadvantaged part of her city (lacking infrastructure, and the dilapidated home to the socially underprivileged), and secondly, to tell a story about mothers and hope – all Rhonda has is the children she was 'blessed' with. (French 2013: n.p.)

And in this final scene Kokkinos reminds us that Rhonda is also 'blessed' with two more children: her eldest Mickey, whose name is written across her hand beside a love heart, and her unborn child, whom she cradles with her hands across her stomach, which Kokkinos draws attention to in a close-up (see Figure 4.2). Reorientated to her children, Rhonda represents the broader 'turn towards' each other, in Ahmed's sense of it, across all of the mother–child relationships of the film. Moreover, with her social worker watching on with genuine care, the scene also raises the possibility of a new start for Rhonda: she is seen, heard, and appears to have the support of an institution she previously

Figure 4.2 Rhonda holding her pregnant stomach in *Blessed*

experienced as antagonist. The latter in particular is a notable shift from both Kokkinos's previous films and from genre conventions, both of which have tended to cast institutions as dangers to the marginalised.

In melodrama, for example, there has been a shift away from the 'natural disaster or the slimy character' and towards 'social institutions' as the villain, and particularly those marked by 'patriarchal laws and class structures' (Gaines 1991: 347). Michael Walker (1982: 35) elaborates that when characters are punished for transgressing these ideologies, which is 'often directed against female characters' with whom the audience are encouraged to empathise, it 'leads to the same sort of sufferings as in traditional melodrama, [but] the ideology' functions 'as the villain'. Similarly, hegemonic institutions are constructed as punishing, or at least failing their most vulnerable constituents in Kokkinos's previous films, as well as in preceding scenes in *Blessed*. For example, in *Head On* the police strip and beat transgendered Toula, while in *The Book of Revelation* the police laugh at Daniel when he attempts to report his abduction.

In *Blessed*, an earlier example occurs when Katrina and Trisha are arrested for shoplifting. The two are dressed in the private school uniforms Trisha stole earlier from her mother Gina. The girls are interviewed by Sergeant Kerrick (played by Neil Pigot), who lectures the girls before concluding with: 'You can't just pretend to be something you're not. [...] And what are you girls? Trash.' His comments reveal that while they were arrested for shoplifting, their larger crime is wearing the stolen uniforms and pretending to be 'something' they are 'not': upper middle class. The moment underscores the hegemonic policing of social divisions and depicts 'what is really at stake in the social politics, not only of the film, but of wider normative societal discourse', which it achieves through a 'symbolic head-to-head between the powers that be: the institutional (in this case, the police), and those that suffer most from institutional exclusion (marginalised working-class youth)' (Hancock 2014: 136). The outsider, realised in *Blessed* across an ensemble of socially marginalised characters, thus again functions as a witness to the failures of hegemonic institutions in the Australian cultural landscape and as a pretext for a critical appraisal of that landscape.

But like many melodramas of protest (and all of Kokkinos's preceding films), *Blessed* also concludes optimistically, offering the redemption of Rhonda as an affirmation of 'the determination to fight on' (Walker 1982: 14). This is most explicitly realised through the penultimate close-up of Rhonda's hands – featuring Mickey's name as she cradles her pregnant stomach – which is the most explicit (and literal) image of hope and rebirth in Kokkinos's oeuvre (see Figure 4.2). That the film ends with Rhonda dancing also reflects another 'motif in Kokkinos' films' (Hopgood 2009: 17). When Vicki dances in *Only the Brave* it introduces Alex's queer gaze; Ari dances throughout *Head On* in a negotiation of his Greek and queer identities; dance is Daniel's livelihood in *The Book of Revelation*, but also a method through which he begins to heal; and in *Blessed*, Bianca dances to drunkenly celebrate the irresponsible purchase of a dress and Rhonda dances in grief. Hopgood (2009: 17) argues that dance functions to 'externalise' these characters' 'inner turmoil and conflict'. While I agree with her persuasive reading, I would add that dance further functions, particularly in key scenes – Ari's final dance, Daniel's recovery dance, Rhonda's final dance – as a symbolic transformation, too. In each of these scenes, there is an attempt through dance to assert (or reassert) an agency lost or challenged in traumatic preceding events. And in this sense, despite what are often read as grim films (for example, Buckmaster 2009), Kokkinos's films consistently end on notes of ambiguous optimism.

An ensemble of outsiders, an oeuvre of outsiders?

Blessed, Kokkinos's third feature (and fifth) film, represents an expanded return to the preoccupations established in her earlier films, *Antamosi*, *Only the Brave*, and *Head On*. Like those films, *Blessed* employs a stylised social realism and sites her characters in a range of primarily working-class milieus, from grim, state-provided apartments to a series of run-down locations. But where those films were typically organised around a single intersectional outsider, *Blessed* disperses these diversities across an ensemble of outsiders. Thus, in *Blessed*, we follow five mothers and their seven children. Though Kokkinos again employs an intersectional focus to her outsiders – Roo is a queer, Greek-Australian youth, for example, while Rhonda is an abused woman and pregnant mother on welfare – it is less emphatically explored or foregrounded here as in *Head On*, which is perhaps inevitable given the number of characters. Nevertheless, in following a series of different mother–child relationships, Kokkinos again insists on approaching Australian identity by emphasising its overlapping and changing plurality.

This plurality is again embodied by the outsider, in this case the mother and child struggling at the margins, with the film's focus largely organised around the impact of this marginalisation on these mothers, their children, and the relationships they share. Like *Antamosi*, *Only the Brave*, and *Head On*, this again culminates in a traumatic experience – the death of two of Rhonda's children – which establishes the outsider as a motif for Kokkinos through which themes of alienation, disaffection, and the powerlessness of the marginalised are explored. That trauma is a uniting experience across Kokkinos's outsiders also foregrounds the vulnerability of the marginalised in often confronting ways, though the subsequent emphasis is typically on empathising with them. This is perhaps unusual (Hancock 2014: 133), but is part of Kokkinos's call (in Mitchell 2017) to '[let] go of judgements and prejudices' of social outsiders. But if *Blessed*'s exploration of an ensemble of outsiders reflects a return to and extension of many of the stylistic and thematic preoccupations established in her earlier films, then to what extent is it possible to read these shared characteristics across her films as evidence of Kokkinos as an auteur?

Notes

1   *Blessed* Production Notes, available at <http://static.thecia.com.au/reviews/b/blessed-production-notes.doc> (last accessed 24 April 2019).
2   Ibid.

Conclusion: an oeuvre of outsiders – an Australian auteur?

I conclude this project by offering some brief notes towards a consideration of Kokkinos as an auteur. That said, Kokkinos's auteur status is perhaps something of a moot point, insomuch as it is one that is occasionally taken for granted. Henry (2014: 125), for example, notes Kokkinos's 'own auteur status' in passing, while Daniel White and Gina Lambropoulos (2017) describe her as an 'Australian auteur'. However, the auteur label is neither one that is widespread nor one that has received focused consideration outside of Ross's (2012: 51) analysis of the soundscape in two of Kokkinos's five fictional films 'within something of an auteur framework'. In that instance, though, it is to allow for a more 'straightforward analysis' by focusing on Kokkinos rather than the 'ensemble of sound designers' (Ross 2012: 51). In this chapter, then, I conclude my survey of Kokkinos's oeuvre by foregrounding the features across, rather than within, her films to begin a conversation about whether (and why) we might consider her an auteur.

Of course, the 'auteur', or notion of the director as a film's defining influence or 'author', is something of an out-of-fashion concept among film scholars. Though there were important precedents (Hayward 2006), the term is perhaps most associated with *Cahiers du Cinéma* writers' development of the *politique des auteurs* in the 1950s and 1960s (for example, Truffaut [1954] 2008; Bazin [1957] 2008). Early scholarship applied the concept to directors with an 'individuality of style', which was often assessed in relation to mise en scène (Truffaut [1954] 2008; Bazin [1957] 2008). By the early 1960s, however, American critics like

Andrew Sarris had shifted the focus and 'reformulated *Cahiers'* *politique* as the "*auteur* theory", transforming the original polemic for a new cinema of *auteurs* into a critical method for evaluating films' (Cook 1985: 114; see Sarris [1962] 2008, 1963). In the intervening decades, 'auteur theory' has faced a multitude of reformations, revisions, and criticisms (Caughie 2007), largely precipitated by a shift away from romanticised notions of the 'artist' and towards a post-structuralist discourse of the 'death of the author' (Barthes 1977). One of the results of this has been a more concerted investigation of film as a collaborative rather than solo production (Staiger 2003),[1] particularly in relation to industrial mainstream (rather than independent) filmmaking like Hollywood where the 'collaborative nature of the business has always put limits on the freedom of the director to claim the status of especially privileged author' (King 2002: 87). Other key criticisms have included feminist concerns about the historically androcentric foci in auteur theory, perhaps most famously articulated by Sharon Smith's (1972: 21) description of it as the 'most incredible of all male fantasies'.

But despite the important criticisms and its wavering scholarly popularity, Adrian Martin (2001: n.p.) argues that auteur theory 'has never really gone away in practice'. Martin (2001: n.p.) notes that what he terms 'classical auteurism' is, in fact, both a 'proposition' that the director can be 'pinpointed as the one most responsible for its art and craft' as well as a 'good way to explore and interpret films [. . .] through focusing on the "signature" or traces of the director's style, "vision" and recurring concerns'. It is not, he insists, the only way to look at a director's oeuvre, but it remains a useful method among many (Martin 2001: n.p.). In similar ways, Doty (1993: 18) has argued that an auteur is a director who 'expressed consistent, idiosyncratic stylistic and thematic concerns throughout the body of their films'. These dual textual emphases on consistent stylistic and thematic preoccupations remain the 'classical' (Martin 2001) or 'traditional' (Doty 1993) conceptions of the auteur; they are also conceptions that Kokkinos is well placed to fulfil.

Kokkinos's films are 'consistently idiosyncratic' (to adapt Doty 1993): for example, they individually and collectively explore her 'vision of Melbourne' from the perspective of outsider protagonists (French 2013: n.p.). Indeed, like the 'auteur films of Mina Shum set in Vancouver or Léa Pool's films set in Montréal' (Melnyk 2014: 79), Kokkinos's fictional films are all set (and filmed) in her home town of Melbourne. While this can presumably be partly understood as convenience or pragmatism, it nevertheless also reflects an active artistic choice. For instance, Kokkinos wrote or co-wrote screenplays set in Melbourne (*Antamosi, Only the Brave*); adapted Melbourne-based literary sources (*Head On, Blessed*); and transposed an Amsterdam-based literary source to Melbourne (*The Book of Revelation*). Melbourne thus 'emerges as a character or signifier of meaning in her films' (French 2013: n.p.) with the culturally diverse but cinematically indistinct city grounding key themes and functioning emblematically of Australian society (see Introduction) across her films. There is also a consistency within this broader setting, with Kokkinos privileging exclusively urban and suburban spaces that often symbolise the interiority of her characters (French 2012, 2013): abandoned shacks, urban back alleys, run-down houses in outer suburbs – sites isolated from mainstream society. This points to a level of 'consistent idiosyncrasy' in setting across Kokkinos's oeuvre. Perhaps more significantly, this recurring setting also signals how heavily Kokkinos is involved in the development of her films, whether as a writer (*Antamosi*), co-writer (*Only the Brave, Head On, The Book of Revelation*), or executive producer (*Blessed*) (Cordaiy 2009). Conceptions of the auteur often rely on a sense that films are 'extensively guided by a director from script to completion' (Tregde 2013: 6), and this is true of Kokkinos. Even with *Blessed*, as the only one of her films that she did not participate in writing, Kokkinos still actively directed its development. Kokkinos notes of the process:

> When we started the adaptation process we kept all the writers on board. We did a couple of drafts and each writer dramatised their own story. Those early drafts were

interesting but they weren't hanging together as a film. So I took a step back and had a think about what to do, and went back to my original emotional response to the play [...] and I remember[ed] the line Rhonda says, 'They are my blessings and you are not to touch them', and I thought, every child is a mother's blessing. So I went back to Andrew [...] and I said 'This story is about mothers and children. There's something about the way all of these characters can speak to each other that we haven't brought out into the open, or haven't emphasised as a theme ... the core theme. (Kokkinos qtd in Cordaiy 2009: 19)

As Mitchell (2017: n.p.) points out, Kokkinos's changes are 'substantially different' from the original play: 'Some characters were discarded, some created or enhanced, and other character connections were introduced.' McFarlane (2010: 87), too, notes Kokkinos's uniting 'vision' in the film: these 'five diverse plot strands, with no more than vestigial connections [...] are woven rigorously together by the coherence and compassion of Kokkinos' vision'. In this way, Kokkinos's hand in actively shaping all of her scripts is consistent with notions of the auteur as 'controlling or otherwise influencing the form and meanings' of their films (Doty 1993: 18).

These 'consistent, idiosyncratic' choices are also reflected in Kokkinos's 'stylistic and thematic concerns' (Doty 1993: 18). In terms of style, for example, Kokkinos employs a stylised realism alongside symbolic uses of colour in each of her films (blues and greys in *Antamosi* and *Only the Brave*; yellows, oranges, and reds in *Head On*, *The Book of Revelation*, and *Blessed*). In *Blessed*, for example, family homes are frequently cast in warm colours, such as deep red curtains and a large yellow poster, reflecting the film's broader 'visual concept' of the 'spectrum of colours within a flame' (Production Notes[2]). This use of colour has symbolic significance, too: James begins the film assessing a fire-damaged building which pre-empts Orton and Stacey's death in a fire at the film's end (see Chapter 4). The latter signals that Kokkinos's films are also united by visceral emphases on trauma – extreme close-ups, disorienting angles, slow motion, and heightened colours and sounds – as with Katina seeing her father's dead body (*Antamosi*), Alex seeing Vicki self-immolate (*Only the Brave*), Ari seeing Toula beaten (*Head On*), Daniel's abduction and torture (*The Book of Revelation*), and Rhonda grieving her children's death (*Blessed*).

These stylistic signatures foreground thematic preoccupations within Kokkinos's oeuvre. That trauma is a uniting experience across her outsiders, for instance, foregrounds Kokkinos's ongoing exploration of the vulnerability of the marginalised which she reveals by privileging the perspective of outsiders, 'all of whom are emotionally vulnerable and scarred by abuse' (French 2013: n.p.). These outsiders are

> frequently *othered*, painfully aware of their difference due to their sexuality (as gays or lesbians); their ethnicity (as Greek immigrants within a troubled multicultural Australia); their socio-economic status (as working class, and often disenfranchised youths); and their place as sons and daughters battling familial tensions (particularly as 2nd generation migrants). (French 2013: n.p.)

In *Antamosi, Only the Brave,* and *Head On,* for example, Kokkinos foregrounds an outsider protagonist who is marked by their location within working-class, Greek-Australian milieus. To this intersectionality she adds, in *Only the Brave* and *Head On,* protagonists who are also young and queer. In *Blessed,* Kokkinos expands this focus to an ensemble of mostly working-class outsiders, most of whom are young and some of whom are also queer (Roo) and/or Greek-Australian (Roo, Trisha, Gina). In *The Book of Revelation,* however, Kokkinos takes a different approach to the outsider. Instead of focusing on a multiply marginalised protagonist that typically offers some kind of disruption to hegemonic conceptions of Australian identity, Kokkinos forcibly removes the white, hetero-masculine Daniel's privilege through trauma. Daniel is remade into an outsider to his own life, leaving his previous life of success and advantage. Instead, Daniel changes his name, leaves his girlfriend and apartment, quits dancing in the city for a stereotypically transitional or working-class job (bartender) on the outskirts of town, and begins pursuing strangers in a wholly ineffective revenge campaign before being literally removed from society through police imprisonment (see Chapter 3). Thus, where Katina, Alex, Ari, and the *Blessed* ensemble all reflect Kokkinos's focus on marginalised or 'othered' characters, *The Book of Revelation* offers the reverse by 'othering' the standard hero of much Australian cinema, namely the white, heterosexual, Anglo-Irish man (Seco 2008).

Across Kokkinos's oeuvre, then, each of her films offers a challenge or disruption to hegemonic conceptions of Australian identity, which are embodied by the figure of the outsider. In this way, the figure of the outsider consistently functions both as a motif through which to explore themes of alienation, disaffection, and the powerless of the marginalised, and as a witness to the failures of institutions in the Australian cultural landscape (with families, schools, and the police the typical targets). As Bazin ([1957] 2008: 25) famously argued, auteurs 'always tell the same story, or, in case the word "story" is confusing, let's say they have the same attitude and pass the same moral judgements on the action and on the characters'. Certainly if the combination of 'distinctive thematic concerns' and a 'distinctive style' that reflects those 'thematic concerns' across a 'director's body of work' is what 'makes a filmmaker an auteur' (King 2002: 87), then Kokkinos is well placed. Interestingly, these recurrent foci are, to some degree, reinforced through casting. Like many auteurs, Kokkinos recasts her actors across multiple films with Elena Mandalas, Dora Kaskanis, Alex Papps, George Harlem, Neil Pigot, and Eugenia Fragos, among others, all appearing in at least two of her films, and imbuing her oeuvre with both an inter- and intra-textuality. Pigot, for instance, plays an abusive (albeit differently named) police officer in both *Head On* and *Blessed*, while Harlem plays damaging Greek-Australian husbands/fathers in *Antamosi* and *Only the Brave*.

Kokkinos's thematic preoccupations also suggest a personal undertone to her oeuvre (French 2012), a 'personal' vision having often been seen as one of the 'central tenets' of conceptions of the auteur (Yoshimoto 2000: 55; Polan 2001). Although Kokkinos has rejected a reading of her oeuvre as autobiographical, she has said a number of times that one of her motivations for becoming a filmmaker was that she had yet to see films that reflected her own personal experience (for example, White and Lambropoulos 2017). In this way, her films reflect 'expositions of her own background', albeit inevitably to different degrees (French 2012: 66). In a radio interview, for example, Kokkinos noted:

> Because I was never mainstream, I was Greek, came from a working-class background, that immigrant experience made me an outsider automatically. My sexuality made me an outsider. [. . .] How that makes you feel as a person when you feel you are not really part of the mainstream. And all of my films, I think, have touched on that, about engaging identity and how one belongs. [. . .] So ironically one struggles with being an outsider and yet, on some level, I think I've also celebrated that outsider status in all my films. (Kokkinos in White and Lambropoulos 2017: n.p.)

This statement sums up many of the issues Kokkinos has raised in other interviews (for example, Stamocostas 2018; Malone 1999; Katsigiannis 1998) and is interesting for a number of reasons. For one thing, it acknowledges many of the preoccupations of her films – Greek-Australian, working-class, queer outsiders – as located in her personal background. For another, it encourages a reading of her oeuvre as thematically consistent given her note that it is characterised by a 'celebration' of 'that outsider status in all' of her films. In other words, Kokkinos is framing herself as an auteur with a uniting personal vision. This is consistent with Staiger's (2003) discussion of the auteur as a 'technique of self'. In this model, the auteur is 'reconceptualized as a subject having an ability to act as a conscious analyzer of the functionality of citations in historical moments' (Staiger 2003: 49). Kokkinos's interviews, such as the one quoted from above, thus become a 'performative statement' as a 'citation of authoring by an individual having the authority to make an authoring statement' (Staiger 2003: 51). This is important because 'authorship does matter [...] especially to those in nondominant positions' – as with Kokkinos as a queer, Greek-Australian woman – because asserting 'agency' can be seen as a 'survival' project and an opportunity to undermine 'naturalized privileges of normativity' (Staiger 2003: 27).

Certainly women, queers, and ethnically marked filmmakers (among other sites of difference) are frequently excluded from the category of 'auteur'. Early discussions of auteurs focused exclusively on male directors and most recent discussions of auteurs still rarely feature, let alone feature prominently, women directors (Jaikumar 2017). This is perhaps particularly true of Australian cinema, which has historically been slow to embrace the notion of the auteur, and even slower to confer that title upon marginalised directors. O'Regan (1996: 125) notes that where Australian directors are discussed as 'auteurs' it is typically seen as an 'exception' that occurs only after they have achieved considerable recognition outside of Australia and, in particular, within North America. While this arguably points to an institutionalised cultural cringe – the notion that Australian culture can only be valued when it is first validated by those outside Australian culture (and particularly by those in the United States or, to a lesser extent, Britain) – a handful of directors have made the grade, including one woman. Oscar-winner Jane Campion, 'Australasia's most high-profile and lionized auteur director' (O'Regan 1996: 288), is a case in point. Kokkinos, however, has actively eschewed international (and specifically North American) opportunities. Kokkinos (in Usher 2006) has talked, for example, about receiving multiple offers to make films in Hollywood after the success of *Head On* but in wanting to stay in Australia and make films 'important to [her]'.

If we accept that Kokkinos is, at the level of her texts, an auteur – 'consistently idiosyncratic' in style and theme – it is perhaps curious that she is not also an obvious auteur candidate at the level of discourse, outside of her self-citations and the handful of writers who (as noted earlier) have described her as such. The auteur is, of course, also a discursive construction influenced, for example, by the 'discourse produced by film critics and scholars who function, in effect, as reputation entrepreneurs' (Allen and Lincoln 2004: 871) or 'reputation builders' (Klinger 1994: xiii). Beyond idiosyncratic textual consistencies, the 'auteur' is thus also discursively conferred – constructed through repeated utterances – revealing the 'dialogic function between artistic reputations and history – the dynamic circumstances under which an author's status and the status of her or his works are established, sustained, transformed, unappreciated, or even vilified' (Klinger 1994: xiii). A director is more likely to be discursively constructed as an 'auteur' when they are the subject of a greater amount of critical attention, such as by being the subject of a greater number of reviews, articles, and books (Allen and Lincoln 2004: 881). Yet, there has been an oft-noted paucity of writing focused on Kokkinos (Hardwick 2009; Collins and Davis 2004; Berry 1999), which can be partly understood in relation to her eschewal of a higher profile and international opportunities. But it is perhaps also understood as a result of a 'critical neglect' that has been raised as potentially related to the challenging depictions of multiple sites of difference in her work (Berry 1999: 35). In discussing *Head On*, ironically Kokkinos's most high-profile and written-about film, Berry writes:

> Some have suggested to me that it is precisely this very marked ethnic and gay combination that has led to critical neglect of [*Head On*]. They have pointed out that since nearly all of Australia's prominent film critics are Anglo and straight, and most of them are male, they could not be expected to grasp a film like *Head On*. (Berry 1999: 35)

Or perhaps, in a national cinema at least historically organised around white, heterosexual men (Berry 1999), a director like Kokkinos. In a recent interview, Kokkinos notes:

> Making features as a Greek Australian lesbian woman that are provocative, emotionally intense: when you think about my films it's almost a miracle they got made. To make four features in this country is quite an achievement. I'm really proud of each and every one of my four features. That only happened through sheer persistence, hard work and being driven by wanting to say something and also wanting to make a cultural contribution to the landscape. (Kokkinos in Stamocostas 2018)

When asked if she has 'paid a price' for her provocative explorations of diverse protagonists and milieus, she notes:

> Have I paid a price? I'm not sure that I have in the sense [that] I wanted to make those films. I wanted to feel that there was a freedom in making those films and I don't have any regrets at all. *I certainly copped a lot of flak*. That's the role of the artist, to pose questions, to take us out of our comfort zone. To explore issues and questions that almost feel slightly forbidden in some way. That's also the role of the storyteller in society, to provoke us into thinking about things more deeply and differently. (Kokkinos in Stamocostas 2018; emphasis added)

Though Kokkinos does not elaborate in the interview on what constitutes 'flak', or whether it was at the hands of reviewers, peers, industry stakeholders, or others, it is nevertheless clear that there has been something of a 'cost'. Certainly it is true that Kokkinos, despite being a celebrated filmmaker, has found it increasingly difficult to secure funding to make films in the government-funded Australian film industry. Her final film was only completed through the personal financial contributions of Kokkinos herself and producer Al Clark (Gonzalez 2009) and, though *Blessed* generally received strong reviews, Kokkinos's directing opportunities have since lain exclusively in television rather than film (White and Lambropoulos 2017).

If we thus see the paucity in discourse around Kokkinos as partly a result of her decision to eschew an international or mainstream career and partly as a result of a broader national reticence around an outsider filmmaker focused on outsider provocations, then it also becomes possible to see her consideration as an auteur as something of a reclamation. Robert Sinnerbrink writes of marginalised filmmakers:

> there is also an *ethical* decision at stake in devoting time and thought to films that deliberately take the path less chosen [. . .]. In a global cultural and economic marketplace dominated by certain types of stories or ideological points of views, there is ethical purpose in devoting attention to the more marginal, more questioning, more aesthetically and intellectually demanding films that one encounters. (Sinnerbrink 2011: 137–8)

Applying Sinnerbrink's (2011) proposition of an ethical imperative to the question of the auteur, the question here might become: to what extent should the comparative discursive paucity devoted to Kokkinos actually matter in considerations of her as an auteur? Evidence of marginalisation should certainly not be permitted to justify further marginalisation. In her compelling consideration of women auteurs, Priya Jaikumar (2017: 206) writes that: 'Authorship was a coveted and near-impossible goal for those who did not fit normative prescriptions of what authors should look like, and what they should make in order [to] find institutional, critical, and popular acceptance.' In the absence of such 'acceptance', we might instead note Patricia White's (2015: 3) account of how 'feminists have explored the work that has been made by women as an act of historical retrieval' and a 'practical matter of equity'. It is thus not only possible to read Kokkinos as an auteur – as a director whose oeuvre is characterised by 'consistent idiosyncrasies' of style, theme, and personal vision, and who is also regularly engaged in 'techniques of self' – but, for me, something of an act of reclamation to do so. And if these short notes are to contribute to anything, it is to offer a starting point for larger conversations not only about the work of Kokkinos, but about that of other nondominant directors, including within the privileged discourse of the 'auteur'. It is thus also a 'call to action' to 'question the authorship of our film industries, our policies, our states, our theories' which promise to reveal 'how the norms and productive conditions of authorship have been working for and against' directors like Kokkinos 'the world over' (Jaikumar 2017: 212).

Ana Kokkinos: an auteur of outsiders

Ana Kokkinos is an Australian screenwriter, producer, and director best known for her work directing fictional films, including the short *Antamosi* (1991), short feature *Only the Brave* (1994), and features *Head On* (1998), *The Book of Revelation* (2006), and *Blessed* (2009). In this book, I have offered a reading of and across these films through the broad focus of tracing the deployment of the outsider as a textual motif and discursive formation. In doing so, I have suggested a reading of Kokkinos's fictional films as an 'oeuvre of outsiders' and Kokkinos herself as an auteur, the latter in both the classical and 'techniques of self' conceptions. But one of the issues the preceding discussions have revealed is that, in many ways, the issues of marginality and invisibility that Kokkinos's outsider characters face in her films are the very same issues she has faced in achieving recognition of her work. Certainly, if there is only one task that this book can be put to, then I hope that it is in contributing to an increased focus on Ana Kokkinos and her oeuvre. And there is considerable work left to do: in expanding on the starting points offered here; in considering her interventions into Greek-Australian milieus as a specifically transnational auteurism; and in widening the focus of studies to consider her by now significant body of work in television, among others.

Notes

1   For a detailed account of the rise and fall of 'auteurism' in film theory, see Lapsley and Westlake (2006: 105–28); see also John Caughie (2007).
2   *Blessed* Production Notes, available at <http://static.thecia.com.au/reviews/b/blessed-production-notes.doc> (last accessed 24 April 2019).

Bibliography

Aaron, Michele (2004), 'New Queer Cinema: An introduction', in Michele Aaron (ed.), *New Queer Cinema: A Critical Reader*, Edinburgh: Edinburgh University Press, pp. 3–14.

Ahmed, Sara (2006), *Queer Phenomenology: Orientations, Objects, Others*, London: Duke University Press.

Allen, Michael Patrick and Anne E. Lincoln (2004), 'Critical discourse and the cultural consecration of American films', *Social Forces* 82.3: 871–93.

Aquilia, Pieter (2001), 'Wog drama and "white multiculturalists": The role of non-Anglo-Australian film and television drama in shaping a national identity', *Journal of Australian Studies* 25.67: 103–8.

Arendell, Terry (1999), 'Hegemonic motherhood: Working paper no. 9', Centre for Working Families, Berkeley: University of California.

Atewologun, Doyin, Ruth Sealy and Susan Vinnicombe (2016), 'Revealing intersectional dynamics in organizations: Introducing intersectional identity work', *Gender, Work and Organization* 23.3: 223–47.

Australian Government (n.d.). 'Abolition of the "White Australia" policy – Fact sheet', Australian Government – Department of Home Affairs, <https://archive.homeaffairs.gov.au/about/corporate/information/fact-sheets/08abolition> (last accessed 12 April 2019).

Australian Government (1989), *National Agenda for a Multicultural Australia*, <http://www.multiculturalaustralia.edu.au/doc/multoff_3.pdf> (last accessed 24 April 2019).

Bahk, Y.-C., S.-K. Jang, K.-H. Choi and S.-H. Lee (2017), 'The relationship between childhood trauma and suicidal ideation: Role of maltreatment and potential mediators', *Psychiatry Investigation* 14.1: 37–43.

Barber, Lynden (1998), 'Reel women', *The Weekend Australian*, 25–6 April, pp. 4–6.

Barlow, Dominic (2015), 'Review of Blessed', *Fourth Reel Film* 4.3, <https://fourthreefilm.com/2015/03/blessed-dir-ana-kokkinos-2009/> (last accessed 12 April 2019).

Barthes, Roland (1977), *Image-Music-Text*, New York: Hill and Wang.

Bazin, Andre [1957] (2008), 'De la politique des auteurs', in Barry Keith Grant (ed.), *Auteurs and Authorship: A Film Reader*, London: Blackwell, pp. 19–28.

Beirne, Rebecca (2012), 'Teen lesbian desires and identities in international cinema: 1931–2007', *Journal of Lesbian Studies* 16.3: 258–72.

Bennett, James (2007), '*Head On*: Multicultural representations of Australian identity in 1990s national cinema', *Studies in Australasian Cinema* 1.1: 61–78.

Berry, Chris (1995), 'Not necessarily *The Sum of Us*: Australia's not-so-queer cinema', *Metro Magazine* 101: 12–16.

Berry, Chris (1999), 'The importance of being Ari', *Metro Magazine* 118: 34–7.

Biggs, Michael (2012), 'Self-immolation in context, 1963–2012', *Revue d'Etudes Tibétaines* 25: 143–50, <https://info-buddhism.com/Self-Immolation-in-Context_Biggs.html> (last accessed 12 April 2019).

Bordwell, David and Kristin Thompson (1997), *Film Art: An Introduction*, international edn, London: McGraw Hill.

Brah, Avtar and Ann Phoenix (2004), 'Ain't I a woman? Revisiting intersectionality', *Journal of International Women's Studies* 5.3: 75–86.

Bronski, Michael (2000), 'Positive images and the coming out film: The art and politics of gay and lesbian cinema', *Cineaste* 26.1: 20–6.

Brooks, Karen (1999), 'Homosexuality, homosociality, and gender blending in Australian film', *Antipodes* 13.2: 85–90.

Buckmaster, Luke (2009), 'Interview with Ana Kokkinos', *Crikey*, 15 September, <http://blogs.crikey.com.au/cinetology/2009/09/15/interview-with-ana-kokkinos-director-of-blessed/> (last accessed 12 April 2019).

Buckmaster, Luke (2014), '*Head On* rewatched', *The Guardian*, 19 September, <https://www.theguardian.com/film/2014/sep/19/head-on-rewatched-hot-blooded-and-hyper-styled-social-realism> (last accessed 12 April 2019).

Butler, Judith (1993), *Bodies That Matter*, New York: Routledge.

Byrnes, Paul (n.d.a) 'Curator's notes: *The Book of Revelation*', *Australian Screen*, <https://aso.gov.au/titles/features/the-book-of-revelation/notes/> (last accessed 12 April 2019).

Byrnes, Paul (n.d.b) 'Curator's notes: *Head On*', *Australian Screen*, <https://aso.gov.au/titles/features/head-on/notes/> (last accessed 12 April 2019).

Byrnes, Paul (n.d.c), 'Curator's notes: *Only the Brave*', *Australian Screen*, <https://aso.gov.au/titles/short-features/only-the-brave/notes/> (last accessed 12 April 2019).

Callahan, David (2001), 'His natural whiteness: Modes of ethnic presence and absence in some recent Australian films', in Ian Craven (ed.), *Australian Cinema in the 1990s*, London: Frank Cass, pp. 95–114.

Caputo, Raffaelle (1993), 'Coming of age: Notes toward a re-appraisal', *Cinema Papers* 94: 12–16.

Caughie, John (2007), 'Authors and auteurs: The uses of theory', in James Donald and Michael Renov (eds), *The SAGE Handbook of Film Studies*, London: Sage, pp. 408–42.

Cerbone, David R. (2006), *Understanding Phenomenology*, London: Routledge.

Clover, Carol (1992), *Men, Women, and Chain Saws: Gender in the Modern Horror Film*, Princeton, NJ: Princeton University Press.

Clover, Carol (1993), 'High and low: The transformation of the rape-revenge movie', in Pam Cook and Philip Dodd (eds), *Women and Film: A Sight and Sound Reader*, London: Scarlet Press, pp. 76–85.

Cohen, Claire (2014), *Male Rape is a Feminist Issue*, London: Palgrave Macmillan.

Collins, Felicity (2009), 'Wogboy comedies and the Australian national type', in Catherine Simpson, Renata Murawska and Anthony Lambert (eds), *Diasporas of Australian Cinema*, Bristol: Intellect, pp. 73–82.

Collins, Felicity and Therese Davis (2004), *Australian Cinema After Mabo*, Cambridge: Cambridge University Press.

Conomos, John (2014), 'Other shorelines, or the Greek-Australian cinema', in Catherine Simpson, Renata Murawska and Anthony Lambert (eds), *Diasporas of Australian Cinema*, Bristol: Intellect, pp. 115–24.

Cook, Pam (1985), *The Cinema Book*, London: British Film Institute.

Cordaiy, Hunter (2006), 'The philosophy of the white room: A conversation with Ana Kokkinos about *The Book of Revelation*', *Metro Magazine* 150: 38–42.

Cordaiy, Hunter (2009), 'Tough love: Ana Kokkinos', *Metro Magazine* 162: 18–20.

Craven, Ian (2001), *Australian Cinema in the 1990s*, London: Frank Cass.

Creed, Barbara (1993), *The Monstrous-feminine: Film, Feminism, Psychoanalysis*, London: Routledge.

Crenshaw, Kimberle (1991), 'Mapping the margins: Intersectionality, identity politics, and violence against women of color', *Stanford Law Review* 43.6: 1241–99.

Danks, Adrian (2012), 'Melbourne: City of the imagination', in Neil Mitchell (ed.), *World Film Locations: Melbourne*, Bristol: Intellect, pp. 6–7.

Danks, Adrian (2017), 'Before *On the Beach*: Melbourne on film in the 1950s', *Senses of Cinema* 85 (December), <http://sensesofcinema.com/2017/screening-melbourne/melbourne-on-film-1950s/> (last accessed 12 April 2019).

Davidson, Monica (2015), 'Knocking on a locked door: Women in Australian feature films', *Metro Screen*, <http://metroscreen.org.au/women-in-australian-film/> (last accessed 12 April 2019).

Dermody, Susan and Elizabeth Jacka (eds) (1988a), *The Imaginary Industry: Australian Film in the Late '80s*, North Ryde, NSW: Australian Film, Television & Radio School Publications.

Dermody, Susan and Elizabeth Jacka (1988b), *The Screening of Australia: Anatomy of a National Cinema*, Sydney: Currency Press.

Doty, Alexander (1993), *Making Things Perfectly Queer: Interpreting Mass Culture*, Minneapolis: University of Minnesota Press.

Driscoll, Catherine (2011), *Teen Film: A Critical Introduction*, London: Bloomsbury.

Driver, Susan (2007), 'Girls looking at girls looking for girls: The visual pleasures and social empowerment of queer teen romance flicks', in Timothy Shary and Alexandra Seibel (eds), *Youth Culture in Global Cinema*, Austin: University of Texas Press, pp. 241–55.

Dunks, Glenn (2015), 'After Priscilla: The queer screen twenty-one years on', *Metro Magazine: Media & Education Magazine* 186: 26–31.

Dyer, Richard (ed.) (1977), *Gays and Film*, London: British Film Institute.

Dyer, Richard (1990), *Now You See It: Studies on Lesbian and Gay Film*, London: Taylor & Francis.

Dyer, Richard with Julianne Pidduck (2003), *Now You See It: Studies on Lesbian and Gay Film*, 2nd edn, London: Routledge.

Fischer, Paul (n.d.) 'Review of *Head On*', *Urban Cinephile*, <http://www.urbancinefile.com.au/home/view.asp?a=1406&s=Reviews> (last accessed 12 April 2019).

Francke, Lizzie (1993), 'Dark side', *Sight and Sound* 3.4: 18–19.

Fraser, Benjamin (2015), *Toward an Urban Cultural Studies*, London: Palgrave Macmillan.

Free, Erin (2016), 'Female Aussie directors: *FilmInk*'s faves', *Film Ink*, 10 June, <https://www.filmink.com.au/female-aussie-directors-filminks-faves/> (last accessed 12 April 2019).

Freiberg, Freda and Joy Damousi (2003), 'Engendering the Greek: The shifting representations of Greek identity in Australian cinema 1970–2000', in Lisa French (ed.), *Womenvision: Women and the Moving Image in Australia*, Melbourne: Damned Publishing, pp. 211–22.

French, Lisa (ed.) (2003), *Womenvision: Women and the Moving Image in Australia*, Melbourne: Damned Publishing.

French, Lisa (2007), *Centring the Female: The Articulation of Female Experience in the Films of Jane Campion*, PhD thesis, RMIT, <https://researchbank.rmit.edu.au/eserv/rmit:6369/French.pdf> (last accessed 12 April 2019).

French, Lisa (2012), 'A view from the west: The cinema of Ana Kokkinos', in Neil Mitchell (ed.), *World Film Locations: Melbourne*, Bristol: Intellect, pp. 66–8.

French, Lisa (2013), 'Ana Kokkinos', *Senses of Cinema* 69 (December), <http://sensesofcinema.com/2013/contemporary-australian-filmmakers/ana-kokkinos/> (last accessed 12 April 2019).

French, Lisa (2014), 'The international reception of Australian women filmmakers', *Continuum: Journal of Media & Cultural Studies* 28.5: 654–65.

Gaines, Jane (1991), 'The scar of shame: Skin color and caste in Black silent melodrama', in Marcia Landy (ed.), *Imitations of Life: A Reader on Film and Television Melodrama*, Detroit: Wayne State University Press, pp. 331–48.

Gilbert, Joanne (2004), *Performing Marginality: Humor, Gender, and Cultural Critique*, Detroit: Wayne State University Press.

Gledhill, Christine (1991), 'Signs of melodrama', in Christine Gledhill (ed.), *Stardom: Industry of Desire*, London: Routledge, pp. 210–34.

Goldsmith, Ben (2001), 'All quiet on the western front? Suburban reverberations in recent Australian cinema', in Ian Craven (ed.), *Australian Cinema in the 1990s*, London: Frank Cass, pp. 115–32.

Goldsmith, Ben (2010), 'Introduction: Australian cinema', in Ben Goldsmith and Geoff Lealand (eds), *Directory of World Cinema: Australia and New Zealand*, Bristol: Intellect, pp. 9–21.

Goldsmith, Ben and Mark David Ryan (eds) (2018), *Australian Cinema in the 2000s*, London: Palgrave Macmillan.

Gonzalez, Miguel (2009), '*Blessed*: Counting their blessings', *Mumbrella*, 15 September, <https://mumbrella.com.au/counting-the-blessings-blessed-816> (last accessed 12 April 2019).

Goodwin, Susan and Kate Huppatz (2010), 'The good mother in theory and research: An overview', in Susan Goodwin and Kate Huppatz (eds), *The Good Mother: Contemporary Motherhoods in Australia*, Sydney: Sydney University Press, pp. 1–24.

Gottschall, Kristina (2010), 'Coming of age', in Ben Goldsmith and Geoff Lealand (eds), *Directory of World Cinema: Australia and New Zealand*, Bristol: Intellect, pp. 176–87.

'Greece (Thessaloniki)' (2018), City of Melbourne, State Government of Victoria, Australia, <https://www.melbourne.vic.gov.au/business/doing-business-globally/sister-cities/Pages/sister-cities-alliances.aspx> (last accessed 24 April 2019).

Griffiths, Robin (2011), 'New Queer Cinema, international', in David A. Gerstner (ed.), *Routledge International Encyclopedia of Queer Culture*, London: Routledge, pp. 424–6.

Hall, Sandra (2006), 'Review of *The Book of Revelation*', *Sydney Morning Herald*, 9 September, <http://www.smh.com.au/news/film-reviews/the-book-of-revelation/2006/09/08/1157222308067.html> (last accessed 12 April 2019).

Hall, Stuart (2015), 'Introduction: Who needs identity?', in Stuart Hall and Paul du Gay (eds), *Questions of Cultural Identity*, London: Sage, pp. 1–17.

Hallam, Julia and Margaret Marshment (2000), *Realism and Popular Cinema*, Manchester: Manchester University Press.

Hancock, Grady (2014), *Re-visioning Australian Social Realism through a Feminine Lens*, PhD thesis, Deakin University, <http://dro.deakin.edu.au/eserv/DU:30067336/hancock-re-visioning-2014A.pdf> (last accessed 24 April 2019).

Hardwick, Joe (2009), 'Wanderlust: Genre, sexuality, and identity in Ana Kokkino's *Head On*', *Cultural Studies Review* 15.1: 33–42.

Harris, Hilary (2000), 'Failing "white woman": Interrogating the performance of respectability', *Theatre Journal* 52.2: 183–209.

Hayward, Susan (2006), *Cinema Studies*, 3rd edn, London: Routledge.

Heller-Nicholas, Alexandra (2011a), 'Fair games and wasted youth: Twenty-five years of Australian rape-revenge films', *Metro Magazine* 170: 86–9.

Heller-Nicholas, Alexandra (2011b), *Rape-Revenge Films: A Critical Study*, London: McFarland.

Henderson, Scott (2007), 'Youth, sexuality, and the nation: *Beautiful Thing* and *Show Me Love*', in Timothy Shary and Alexandra Siebel (eds), *Youth Culture in Global Cinema*, Austin: University of Texas Press, pp. 256–70.

Henry, Claire (2013), 'Challenging the boundaries of cinema's rape-revenge genre in *Katalin Varga* and *Twilight Portrait*', *Studies in European Cinema* 10.2 & 3: 133–45.

Henry, Claire (2014), *Revisionist-Rape-Revenge*, London: Palgrave Macmillan.

Hopgood, Fincina (2006), '*The Book of Revelation*: Showing without telling', *Metro Magazine* 150: 33–6.

Hopgood, Fincina (2009), 'Thinking through tears: Mothers and children in *Blessed*', *Metro Magazine* 162: 14–17.

Howson, Richard (2006), *Challenging Hegemonic Masculinity*, London: Routledge.

Hunn, Deborah (2000), '"It's not that I can't decide; I don't like definitions": Queer in Australia in Christos Tsiolkas's *Loaded* and Ana Kokkinos's *Head On*', in David Alderson and Linda Anderson (eds), *Territories of Desire in Queer Culture: Refiguring Contemporary Boundaries*, Manchester: Manchester University Press, pp. 112–29.

Hunn, Deborah (2005), 'Australian film', in Claude J. Summers (ed.), *The Queer Encyclopedia of Film and Television*, San Francisco: Cleis Press, pp. 37–9.

Ioannou, Theo (2017), 'Global Greek Diaspora Library to be created in Melbourne', *Greek Reporter*, 17 September, <https://au.greekreporter.com/2017/09/17/global-greek-diaspora-library-to-be-created-in-melbourne/> (last accessed 12 April 2019).

Jagose, Annamarie (1996), *Queer Theory*, Melbourne: University of Melbourne Press.

Jaikumar, Priya (2017), 'Feminist and non-western interrogations of film authorship', in Kristin Lené Hole, Dijana Jelača, E. Ann Kaplan and Patrice Petro (eds), *The Routledge Companion to Cinema and Gender*, London: Routledge, pp. 205–14.

Jancovich, Mark (1996), *Rational Fears: American Horror in the 1950s*, Manchester: Manchester University Press.

Jennings, Ros and Loykie Lominé (2004), 'Nationality and New Queer Cinema: Australian film', in Michele Aaron (ed.), *New Queer Cinema: A Critical Reader*, New Brunswick, NJ: Rutgers University Press, pp. 144–54.

Johnston Deidre and Debra Swanson (2003), 'Invisible mothers: A content analysis of motherhood ideologies and myths in magazines', *Sex Roles* 49: 21–34.

Jorgensen, Darren (2005), 'The new Australian realism', *Metro Magazine* 146/147: 147–51.

Kalina, Paul (2009), 'A passionate take', *The Age*, 10 October, <https://www.theage.com.au/entertainment/movies/a-passionate-take-20091010-ge84yq.html> (last accessed 12 April 2019).

Kaplan, E. Ann [1992] (2013), *Motherhood and Representation: The Mother in Popular Culture and Melodrama*, London: Routledge.

Katsigiannis, Tony (1998), 'Ana Kokkinos: Her journey from Melbourne's western suburbs to Cannes', *Screen Director* (June/July): 6–7.

Kennerson, Elliott (1999), 'Coming up: Alex Dimiatriades', *Out* (June): 35.

Kent, Jacqueline (2010), *The Making of Julia Gillard*, London: Viking.

Khan, Rimi, Danielle Wyatt, Audrey Yue and Nikos Papastergiadis (2013), 'Creative Australia and the dispersal of multiculturalism', *Asia Pacific Journal of Arts and Cultural Management* 10.1 (December): 25–34.

King, Geoff (2002), *New Hollywood Cinema: An Introduction*, New York: Columbia University Press.

Kirkby, Diane (2007), '"Ocker sheilahs" and "bloody barmaids": *Caddie*, biography and gender history in 1970s Australian historical film', *Australian Historical Studies* 38.130: 279–95.

Kitson, Michael (2008), 'From *Gidget* to *Surf Nazis* to *Newcastle*: The genre of the surfing film', *Metro Magazine* 158: 28–31.

Klinger, Barbara (1994), *Melodrama and Meaning: History, Culture, and the Films of Douglas Sirk*, Bloomington and Indianapolis: Indiana University Press.

Knight, Julia (1995), 'The meaning of Treut?', in Tamsin Wilton (ed.), *Immortal, Invisible: Lesbians and Moving Image*, London: Routledge, pp. 34–51.

'Kokkinos, Ana' (n.d.), University of Melbourne, <https://events.unimelb.edu.au/presenters/5786-ana-kokkinos> (last accessed 12 April 2019).

Koleth, Elsa (2010), 'Multiculturalism: A review of Australian policy statements and recent debates in Australia and overseas', Research Paper no. 6 2010–11, Parliament of Australia, <https://www.aph.gov.au/About_Parliament/Parliamentary_Departments/Parliamentary_Library/pubs/rp/rp1011/11rp06#_Toc275248121> (last accessed 12 April 2019).

Krach, Aaron (1999), 'Interviews: "Head On" with Anna [sic] Kokkinos: On Greeks, Queers, and Aussies', *Indiewire*, 12 August, <http://www.indiewire.com/1999/08/interviews-head-on-with-anna-kokkinos-on-greeks-queers-and-aussies-82140/> (last accessed 12 April 2019).

Krauth, Kristen (2009), 'Mothers and children', *RealTime* 93 (Oct.–Nov.): 27.

Kuhn, Annette (1992), 'Woman's genres', in *Screen* (ed.), *The Sexual Subject: A Screen Reader in Sexuality*, London: Routledge, pp. 301–11.

Kunze, Peter (2013), 'Out in the outback: Queering nationalism in Australian film comedy', *Studies in Australasian Cinema* 7.1: 49–59.

Lamble, David (2012), 'Return of the New Queer Cinema', *Bay Area Reporter*, 5 June, <https://www.ebar.com/arts_&_culture/movies//228506> (last accessed 12 April 2019).

Lapsley, Robert and Michael Westlake (2006), *Film Theory: An Introduction*, Manchester: Manchester University Press.

Lawler, Steph (2008), *Identity: Sociological Perspectives*, London: Polity.

Lehman, Peter (2001), *Masculinity: Bodies, Movies, Culture*, New York: Routledge.

Leigh, Jacob (2002), *The Cinema of Ken Loach: Art in the Service of the People*, London: Wallflower Press.

Lindop, Samantha (2015), *Postfeminism and the Fatale Figure in Neo-noir Cinema*, London: Palgrave Macmillan.

Lodge, Guy (2018), 'Why are there so few queer female coming-of-age movies?', *The Guardian*, 1 August, <https://www.theguardian.com/film/2018/aug/01/film-cameron-post-queer-coming-of-age-movies> (last accessed 12 April 2019).

McCann, Andrew (2015), *Christos Tsiolkas and the Fiction of Critique: Politics, Obscenity, Celebrity*, London: Anthem Press.

McFarlane, Brian (1987), *Australian Cinema 1970 – 1985*, London: Secker and Warburg.

McFarlane, Brian (2006), 'The film of the book: Adaptation and the Australian cinema', *Metro Magazine* 149: 52–9.

McFarlane, Brian (2009), 'Resisting Tarantino: A seminal year in Australian cinema', *Australian Book Review* 317: 45–7.

McFarlane, Brian (2010), 'All in the family: Three Australian women directors', *Meanjin Quarterly* 69.3: 82–8.

McIntyre, Joanna (2009), 'Revealing and revolting: Homosexual and transgender panic in two Australian films', *Intersections: Women's and Gender Studies in Review Across Disciplines* 7 (Fall): 40–52.

McIntyre, Joanna (2010), 'Straight places, queer spaces', *Metro Magazine* 165: 82–6.

McWilliam, Kelly (2017a), 'Girl meets girl: Sexual sitings in lesbian romantic comedies', in Gilad Padva and Nurit Buchweitz (eds), *Intimate Relations in Cinema, Literature and Visual Culture*, London: Palgrave Macmillan, pp. 145–55.

McWilliam, Kelly (2017b), ' "It was the summer when everything changed . . .": Coming of age queer in Australian cinema', in Mark David Ryan and Ben Goldsmith (eds), *Australian Screen in the 2000s*, London: Palgrave Macmillan, pp. 191–206.

McWilliam, Kelly and Sharon Bickle (2017), 'Re-imagining the rape-revenge genre: Ana Kokkinos' *The Book of Revelation*', *Continuum: Journal of Media and Cultural Studies* 31.5: 706–13.

McWilliam, Kelly and Mark David Ryan (eds) (forthcoming), *Australian Genre Film*, London: Routledge.

Malone, Peter (1999), 'Interview with Ana Kokkinos', *Peter Malone*, 8 July, <http://petermalone.misacor.org.au/tiki-index.php/tiki-index.php?page=Ana+Kokkinos&bl> (last accessed 12 April 2019).

Mancuso, Luke (2010), '*Brokeback Mountain* and the history of the future of the normal', in JoAnne C. Juett and David M. Jones (eds), *Coming Out to the Mainstream: New Queer Cinema in the 21st Century*, Newcastle upon Tyne: Cambridge Scholars Publishing, pp. 91–124.

Martin, Adrian (2001), 'Sign your name across my heart, or: "I want to write about Delbert Mann" ', *Screening the Past*, <http://www.screeningthepast.com/2014/12/sign-your-name-across-my-heart-or-i-want-to-write-about-delbert-mann/> (last accessed 12 April 2019).

Martin-Jones, David (2009), *Global Cinema: Scotland*, Edinburgh: Edinburgh University Press.

Mayer, David (2018), 'Melodrama in early film', in Carolyn Williams (ed.), *The Cambridge Companion to English Melodrama*, Cambridge: Cambridge University Press, pp. 224–44.

Melnyk, George (2014), *Film and the City: The Urban Imaginary in Canadian Cinema*, Edmonton, AB: AU Press.

Mennel, Barbara (2012), *Queer Cinema: Schoolgirls, Vampires and Gay Cowboys*, London: Wallflower Press.

Mitchell, Jim (2017), 'The ties that bind: The making of *Blessed*', *FilmInk*, 4 August, <https://filmink.com.au/ties-bind-making-blessed/> (last accessed 12 April 2019).

Molloy, Shannon (2016), 'Aussie film and TV is a "sausage fest" where women rarely get a say. This is the $3m plan to change that', *News Corp Australia*, 12 July, <https://www.news.com.au/entertainment/tv/aussie-film-and-tv-is-a-sausage-fest-where-women-rarely-get-a-say-this-

is-the-3m-plan-to-change-that/news-story/154975962843cc0afd1c30fa
b93a905a> (last accessed 12 April 2019).

Monaghan, Whitney (2010), '"It's all in a day's work for a 15-year-old gay
virgin": Coming out and coming of age in teen television', *Colloquy*
19: 56–69, <http://artsonline.monash.edu.au/wp-content/arts-files/
colloquy/colloquy_issue_nineteen/monaghan.pdf> (last accessed 12
April 2019).

Monaghan, Whitney (2017a), 'Girlhood wild and queer: Ana Kokkinos's *Only
the Brave*', *Senses of Cinema* 83 (July), <http://sensesofcinema.com/2017/
pioneering-australian-women/only-the-brave-1994/> (last accessed 12
April 2019).

Monaghan, Whitney (2017b), '*Only the Brave* gaze queerly', *Peephole Journal*
8 (July), <http://peepholejournal.tv/issue/08/07-monaghan/> (last
accessed 12 April 2019).

Moran, Albert and Errol Veith (2005), *Historical Dictionary of Australian and
New Zealand Cinema*, Oxford: Scarecrow Press.

Mulvey, Laura (2013), 'Between melodrama and realism: *Under the Skin of the
City* (2001)', *The Cine-Files* 4 (Spring), <http://www.thecine-files.com/
current-issue-2/guest-scholars/laura-mulvey/> (last accessed 12 April
2019).

Nagel, Joanne (2001), 'Racial, ethnic, and national boundaries: Sexual intersections and symbolic interactions', *Symbolic Interaction* 24.2: 123–39.

Neale, Steve (2004), *Genre and Hollywood*, London: Routledge.

O'Regan, Tom (1987), 'Australian film in the 1950s', *Continuum: Journal of
Media and Cultural Studies* 1.1: n.p., <http://wwwmcc.murdoch.edu.au/
readingroom/film/1950s.html> (last accessed 12 April 2019).

O'Regan, Tom (1995), 'Beyond "Australian film"? Australian cinema in the
1990s', Culture & Communication Reading Room, Murdoch University,
<https://wwwmcc.murdoch.edu.au/ReadingRoom/film/1990s.html>
(last accessed 12 April 2019).

O'Regan, Tom (1996), *Australian National Cinema*, London: Routledge.

O'Regan, Tom (2001), '"Knowing the processes but not the outcomes":
Australian cinema faces the millennium', in Tony Bennett and David Carter
(eds), *Culture in Australia: Policies, Publics and Programs*, Cambridge:
Cambridge University Press, pp. 18–45.

Ozdowski, Sev (2012), 'Australian multiculturalism: The roots of its success',
Conference paper, Third International Conference on Human Rights
Education: Promoting Change in Times of Transition and Crisis, The
Jagiellonian University in Krakow, Poland, 6–10 December, <https://
www.westernsydney.edu.au/equity_diversity/equity_and_diversity/
tools_and_resources/reportsandpubs/australian_multiculturalism_the_
roots_of_its_success> (last accessed 12 April 2019).

Padva, Gilad (2004), 'Edge of seventeen: Melodramatic coming-out in new queer adolescence films', *Communication and Critical/Cultural Studies* 1.4: 355–72.

Padva, Gilad (2014), *Queer Nostalgia in Cinema and Popular Culture*, London: Palgrave Macmillan.

Papanikolaou, Dimitris (2009), 'New queer Greece: Thinking identity through Constantine Giannaris's *From the Edge of the City* and Ana Kokkinos's *Head On*', *New Cinemas: Journal of Contemporary Film* 6.3 (February): 183–96.

Papastergiadis, Nikos (2012), 'Seeing through multicultural perspectives', *Identities: Global Studies in Culture and Power* 19.4: 398–410.

Parkinson, Anna M. (2010), 'Neo-feminist *Mütterfilm*? The emotional politics of Margarethe von Trotta's *Rosentrasse*', in Jaimey Fisher and Brad Pager (eds), *The Collapse of the Conventional: German Film and its Politics at the Turn of the Twenty-First Century*, Detroit: Wayne State University Press, pp. 109–35.

Pascoe, Caroline M. (1998), *Screening Mothers: Representations of Motherhood in Australian Films From 1900 to 1988*, PhD thesis, University of Sydney, <https://ses.library.usyd.edu.au/bitstream/2123/385/3/adt-NU1999.0010whole.pdf> (last accessed 12 April 2019).

Phoenix, Ann and Pamela Pattynama (2006), 'Intersectionality', *European Journal of Women's Studies* 13.3: 187–92.

Plunkett, Felicity (2006), '"You make me a dot in the nowhere": Textual encounters in the Australian immigration story', *Journal of Australian Studies* 30.88: 41–9.

Polan, Dana (2001), 'Auteur desire', *Screening the Past*, <http://www.screeningthepast.com/2014/12/auteur-desire/> (last accessed 12 April 2019).

Pomeranz, Margaret (2011), '3 classic Australian films', *Australian Women's Weekly* 81.3: 248.

Pomeranz, Margaret and David Stratton (2016), '*Head On* review: Shocking, confronting and dazzling', *SBS*, 8 January, <https://www.sbs.com.au/movies/review/head-review-shocking-confronting-and-dazzling> (last accessed 12 April 2019).

Projansky, Sarah (2001), *Watching Rape: Film and Television in Postfeminist Culture*, New York: New York University Press.

Raynor, Jonathan (2000), *Contemporary Australian Cinema: An Introduction*, Manchester: Manchester University Press.

Read, Jacinta (2000), *The New Avengers: Feminism, Femininity, and the Rape-Revenge Cycle*, Manchester: Manchester University Press.

Reimer, Vanessa and Sarah Sahagian (2015), 'Introduction: Contextualizing the mother-blame game', in Vanessa Reimer and Sarah Sahagian (eds), *The Mother-Blame Game*, Bradford, ON: Demeter Press, pp. 1–16.

Reynolds, Robert (1999), 'Living the gay life: Identity and politics in twentieth century Australia', *Island* 77: 53–62.

Rich, B. Ruby (1992), 'New Queer Cinema', *Sight and Sound* 5.2: 30–4.

Romm, Sharon, Heidi Combs and Matthew Klein (2008), 'Self-immolation: Cause and culture', *Journal of Burn Care and Research* 29.6 (November): 988–93.

Ross, Elaine (2012), 'Ana Kokkinos and the auditory spectator', *Screen Sound* 3: 51–66.

Russo, Vito (1981), *The Celluloid Closet: Homosexuality in the Movies*, London: Harper & Row.

Rustin, Emily (2001), 'Romance and sensation in the "glitter cycle"', in Ian Craven (ed.), *Australian Cinema in the 1990s*, London: Frank Cass, pp. 133–49.

Sarris, Andrew (1963), 'The auteur theory and the *Perils of Pauline*', *Film Quarterly* 16.4 (Summer): 26–33.

Sarris, Andrew [1962] (2008), 'Notes on the auteur theory in 1962', in Barry Keith Grant (ed.), *Auteurs and Authorship: A Film Reader*, London: Blackwell, pp. 35–45.

Schubart, Rikke (2007), *Super Bitches and Action Babes: The Female Hero in Popular Cinema, 1970–2006*, Jefferson, NC: McFarland.

Schwartz, Susan (2017), 'The dead father effect on the psyche of a daughter: Sylvia Plath', *Journal of Poetry Therapy* 30.4: 218–27.

Screen Australia (2017), 'Top 100 Australian feature films of all time: Ranked by total reported gross Australian box office', *Screen Australia*, <https://www.screenaustralia.gov.au/fact-finders/cinema/australian-films/top-films-at-the-box-office> (last accessed 12 April 2019).

Seco, Olga (2008), 'Recycling older discourses: The recuperation of the Australian national myth in Elliot's *The Adventures of Priscilla, Queen of the Desert*', in Sara Martin (ed.), *Recycling Culture(s)*, Newcastle upon Tyne: Cambridge Scholars Publishing, pp. 137–46.

Shaw, Jason (2012), *Top 50 Most Influential Gay Movies of All Time*, Lulu.com.

Sinnerbrink, Robert (2011), *New Philosophies of Film: Thinking Images*, London: Bloomsbury.

Smith, Sharon (1972), 'The image of women in film: Some suggestions for future research', *Women and Film* 1: 13–21.

Soltysik, Agnieszka M. (2008), 'Melodrama and the American combat film', in Ralph J. Poole and Ilka Saal (eds), *Passionate Politics: The Cultural Work of American Melodrama from the Early Republic to the Present*, Newcastle upon Tyne: Cambridge Scholars Publishing, pp. 165–86.

Speed, Lesley (1998), 'Tuesday's gone: The nostalgia teen film', *Journal of Popular Film and Television* 26.1: 24–32.

Staiger, Janet (2003), 'Authorship approaches', in David A. Gerstner and Janet Staiger (eds), *Authorship and Film*, New York: Routledge, pp. 27–60.

Stamocostas, Con (2018), 'Interview with Ana Kokkinos', *Neos Kosmos*, 27 November, <https://neoskosmos.com/en/124699/where-is-ana-kokkinos/> (last accessed 12 April 2019).

Stratton, David (2017), [DVD] *Stories of Australian Cinema*, Episode 2: Outsiders, Stranger than Fiction Films.

Tavan, Gwenda (2006), 'John Howard's multicultural paradox', Conference paper, John Howard's Decade Conference, Australian National University, Canberra, 3–4 March, <http://parlinfo.aph.gov.au/parlInfo/search/display/display.w3p;query=Id%3A%22media%2Fpressrel%2FI MYI6%22> (last accessed 12 April 2019).

Thomas, Kevin (1999), 'MOVIES: Collision with life', *LA Times*, 2 September, <https://www.latimes.com/archives/la-xpm-1999-sep-02-ca-5854-story.html> (last accessed 24 April 2019).

Tregde, David (2013), 'A case study on film authorship: Exploring the theoretical and practical sides in film production', *The Elon Journal of Undergraduate Research in Communications* 4.2 (Fall): 5–15.

Truffaut, François [1954] (2008), 'A certain tendency of the French cinema', in Barry Keith Grant (ed.), *Auteurs and Authorship: A Film Reader*, London: Blackwell, pp. 9–18.

Tuccio, Silvana (2008), 'Whose story is reclaimed in *The Home Song Stories*?', *Studies in Australasian Cinema* 2.1: 15–20.

Tziallas, Evangelos (2010), 'Surveillance, space and performance: Informing interstitial subjectivities in *Head On*', *Jump Cut* 52, <http://ejumpcut.org/archive/jc52.2010/evangelosHeadOn/index.html> (last accessed 12 April 2019).

Urban, Andrew (2006), 'Review of *The Book of Revelation*', *Urban Cinephile*, <http://www.urbancinefile.com.au/home/view.asp?a=12187&s=Interviews> (last accessed 12 April 2019).

Usher, Robin (2006), 'A revelation and not by the book', interview with Ana Kokkinos, *The Age*, 29 July, <http://www.theage.com.au/news/film/a-revelation-and-not-by-the-book/2006/07/27/1153816322188.html?page=4> (last accessed 12 April 2019).

Verhoeven, Deb (1997), 'Putting the out:back into the ocker: The sexual terrain of Australian cinema', in Claire Jackson (ed.), *The Bent Lens*, Melbourne: Australian Catalogue Company, pp. 25–32.

Vernay, Jean-François (2006), 'Only disconnect-canonizing homonormative values: Representation and the paradox of gayness in Christos Tsiolkas's *Loaded*', *Antipodes* 20.1, <https://www.questia.com/library/journal/1P3-1303772971/only-disconnect-canonizing-homonormative-values-representation> (last accessed 12 April 2019).

Walker, Michael (1982), 'Melodrama and the American cinema', *Movie* 29/30: 2–38.

Weiss, Andrea (1993), *Vampires and Violets: Lesbians in Film*, London: Penguin Books.

White, Daniel and Gina Lambropoulos (2017), 'Interview with Ana Kokkinos', Out Takes, *Joy* 94.9, 3 August, <https://joy.org.au/outtakes/2017/08/03/a-queer-guide-to-the-melbourne-international-film-festival-with-ana-kokkinos-and-al-cossar/> (last accessed 12 April 2019).

White, Patricia (2015), *Women's Cinema, World Cinema: Projecting Contemporary Feminisms*, Durham, NC: Duke University Press.

Whitman, Walt [1885] (1991), *Selected Poems*, New York: Dover Publications.

Whittaker, Tom (2011), *The Films of Elias Querejeta: A Producer of Landscapes*, Cardiff: University of Wales Press.

Williams, Linda (2011), 'Melodrama', *Oxford Bibliographies Online*, <http://www.oxfordbibliographies.com/view/document/obo-9780199791286/obo-9780199791286-0043.xml> (last accessed 12 April 2019).

Wilton, Tamsin (1995), 'Introduction', in Tamsin Wilton (ed.), *Immortal, Invisible: Lesbians and Moving Image*, London: Routledge, pp. 1–19.

Yoshimoto, Mitsuhiro (2000), *Kurosawa: Film Studies and Japanese Cinema*, Durham, NC: Duke University Press.

Filmography

52 Tuesdays (2013), film. Directed by S. Hyde. Closer Productions.

Acolytes (2008), film. Directed by J. Hewitt. Stewart and Wall Entertainment.

The Adventures of Priscilla, Queen of the Desert (1994), film. Directed by S. Elliot. PolyGram Filmed Entertainment.

All Over Me (1997), film. Directed by A. Sichel. Baldini Pictures.

Antamosi (1991), film. Directed by A. Kokkinos. Victorian College of Arts, <https://www.youtube.com/watch?v=NpPhlRdgeKw> (last accessed 12 April 2019).

Blessed (2009), film. Directed by A. Kokkinos. Blessed Film Productions.

Bloomington (2010), film. Directed by Fernanda Cardoso. Frameline.

The Book of Revelation (2006), film. Directed by A. Kokkinos. Wildheart Zizani.

Braveheart (1995), film. Directed by M. Gibson. Icon Entertainment International.

Brokeback Mountain (2005), film. Directed by A. Lee. Focus Features.

Cracks (2009), film. Directed by J. Scott. Element Pictures.

Death in Brunswick (1990), film. Directed by J. Ruane. Meridian Films.

Deliverance (1972), film. Directed by J. Boorman. Warner Bros Pictures.

Descent (2007), film. Directed by T. Lugacy. City Lights Pictures.

Edge of Seventeen (1998), film. Directed by D. Moreton. Blue Streak Films.

Edward II (1991), film. Directed by D. Jarman. Working Title Films.

Fran (1985), film. Directed by G. Hambly. Barron Films.

Get Real (1998), film. Directed by S. Shore. Distant Horizon.

Head On (1998), film. Directed by A. Kokkinos. Head On Productions.

The Heartbreak Kid (1993), film. Directed by M. Jenkins. Village Roadshow.

I'll Sleep When I'm Dead (2003), film. Directed by M. Hodges. Mosaic Film Group.

The Incredibly True Adventure of Two Girls in Love (1995), film. Directed by M. Maggenti. Fine Line Features.

I Spit on Your Grave (2010), film. Directed by S. R. Monroe. Cinetel Films.

Kill Bill Vol. 1 (2003), film. Directed by Q. Tarantino. Miramax.

Kill Bill Vol. 2 (2004), film. Directed by Q. Tarantino. Miramax.

The Last Days of Chez Nous (1992), film. Directed by G. Armstrong. Offshoot Films.

The Last House on the Left (2009), film. Directed by D. Iliadis. Rogue Pictures.

Lipstick (1976), film. Directed by L. Johnson. Paramount Pictures.

Love and Other Catastrophes (1996), film. Directed by E.-K. Croghan. Fox Searchlight.

Loving Annabelle (2006), film. Directed by K. Brooks. Divine Light Pictures.

Mädchen in Uniform (1931), film. Directed by L. Sagan. Deutsche Film-Gemeinschaft.

Mad Max: Fury Road (2015), film. Directed by G. Miller. Warner Bros Pictures.

Memento (2000), film. Directed by C. Nolan. Newmarket Capital Group.

Monster Pies (2013), film. Directed by L. Galea. Indie Melbourne Productions.

Ms. 45 (1981), film. Directed by A. Ferrara. Navaron Films.

Muriel's Wedding (1994), film. Directed by P. J. Hogan. House and Moorhouse Films.

Newcastle (2008), DVD. Directed by D. Castle. Wolfe Video.

Only the Brave (1994), VHS. Directed by A. Kokkinos. Pickpocket Productions.

The Original Mermaid (2002), film. Directed by M. Cordell and A. Kokkinos. Hilton Cordell and Associates.

Poison (1991), film. Directed by T. Haynes. Bronze Eye Productions.

Radiance (1998), film. Directed by R. Perkins. Eclipse Films.

Show Me Love (1998), film. Directed by L. Moodysson. Memfis Film.

Straw Dogs (2011), film. Directed by R. Lurie. Battleplan Productions.

Strictly Ballroom (1992), film. Directed by B. Luhrmann. M&A Productions.

The Sum of Us (1994), film. Directed by G. Burton and K. Dowling. Samuel Goldwyn.

Sweetie (1989), film. Directed by J. Campion. Filmpac Distribution.

Swoon (1992), film. Directed by T. Kalin. Intolerance Productions.

Talk (1994), film. Directed by S. Lambert. Suitcase Films.

Tan Lines (2006), film. Directed by E. Alridge. Midget Pictures.

Teeth (2007), film. Directed by M. Lichtenstein. Pierpoline Films.

The Virgin Spring (1960), film. Directed by I. Bergman. Svensk Filmindustri.

Vulgar (2000), film. Directed by B. Johnson. Chango Productions.

Waiting (1991), film. Directed by J. McKimmie. Filmside Productions.

Index